The Saviour's Invitation

The Saviour's Invitation

and Other Evangelistic Sermons

By

HYMAN APPELMAN

Author, *"Ye Must Be Born Again,"*
God's Answer to Man's Sin

SECOND EDITION

BAKER BOOK HOUSE
Grand Rapids, Michigan

PHOTOLITHOPRINTED BY CUSHING - MALLOY, INC.
ANN ARBOR, MICHIGAN, UNITED STATES OF AMERICA
1975

To

My beloved pastor

C. E. MATTHEWS

A source of constant challenge
and inspiration

Pastor, Travis Avenue Baptist Church
Fort Worth, Texas

PREFACE

These sermons were *preached*, not written, not edited, but preached in burning anxiety, in pleading earnestness, in yearning appeal for the salvation and consecration of souls. They were born of sleepless nights and agony-filled days. They lay claim to no originality either in thought, outline or contents.

Reader, judge them not as oratorical, rhetorical, grammatical compositions. They are the blood, the sweat, the tears, the hope, the faith of this humble preacher. God has been pleased to use them in the Holy Spirit. They are, every one of them, sent out humbly, by request. If the reading of them will stir one life for Christ, the evangelist will be more than repaid.

May the Holy Spirit of God use them for the glory of the Lord Jesus Christ, for the discomfiting of Satan, for the salvation of souls.

HYMAN J. APPELMAN

Fort Worth, Texas

CONTENTS

CONTENTS

I
THE NEEDED REVIVAL

Wilt thou not revive us again: that thy people may rejoice in thee? (Ps. 85:6)

Some people think the need for a revival is a sign of decadence in a church. This is not always so. In the New Testament, in the Old Testament, in Christian history, revivals have been a part of God's plan for the advancement of the kingdom. This is natural. This is spiritual. This is psychological. It is impossible for a farmer to be always harvesting. The same is true of the Lord's work. We cannot have a perennial revival. It is impossible to have a perpetual harvest, physical or spiritual. We are so constituted that it is impossible for us to be always on the heights. We would go mad with the strain. We could not endure it. The flesh is still with us.

What many people call revivals are not revivals at all. You have heard of revivals with supposedly great singing, with supposedly great preaching — and with few if any noticeable results. Such meetings are not revivals. They may be extended seasons of singing and preaching, but that is all. A revival is a revival. You do not have to be told you were born. You know it. You were there, not consciously, but you were there. The same is true of a revival. You will know it. You will witness it when it comes. Mere preaching is not enough. We want something that will make people know there is a God in heaven, that the Bible is His Word, that the promises of God are yea and amen in Christ. A real revival shakes, breaks, melts, molds, causes the power of God to flow over the hearts of people. We want a revival.

God is ready to give it. He wants us to have it. He will give us that kind of victory the minute we make room for it. How can we make room for God? That is our present and pressing problem. Let us therefore consider the purpose of a revival, the personnel of a revival and the price of a revival.

The first purpose of a revival is to expose sin in the hearts and lives of God's people and in the hearts and lives of the unsaved multitudes. You know without my telling you that when workmen build a giant skyscraper, the higher they go the deeper they must go. As the walls go higher, the basements and subbasements go deeper. The same is true of a revival. To build a structure for the glory of God and the salvation of the lost, you must dig, blast and carry away all those things which might hinder progress. I can say by experience — thank God, I can witness to you of personal knowledge — that nothing can convict of sin, condemn for sin, bring people faster and more definitely to a realization of their sins than a revival of religion.

There has never been so much gambling, drinking, adultery, corruption in high places and in low as there is now. Immorality, indecency, infidelity are rife. How we need to expose the rottenness, the evil, the corruption in the hearts of all the people! We go on day after day, month after month, year after year, in the even or uneven tenor of our ways. Sin becomes so common, so prevalent that we pay no attention to it. We have every sort of philosophical and psychological explanation. "Everybody does it." Our consciences are dead. Our minds are befogged by Satan. We have grown fat and sleek in our souls. We love to hear soft, warm, perfumed platitudes. We need a shock of terrific dynamite to blast us out of the rut into which the Devil has thrown us. The only kind of explosion that can accomplish this is a Holy Ghost revival.

The second purpose of a revival is to enlist souls. First we must seek to enlist God's people. Why are our churches half empty? Why do not souls come to Christ? Because Christians are not sufficiently concerned about the work of the Lord. We have to enlist God's people. We must enlist those who are twice born, who are washed in the blood, who have been regenerated by the Holy Spirit, who claim the Lord as their personal Saviour.

We must enlist also the unsaved, bring them out of darkness into light, lead them from hell to heaven, from sin to salvation, from iniquity to righteousness. We must win them for the Lord Jesus Christ. The majority of people who have been saved since the beginning of Christianity have been reached and enlisted during revival meetings. The majority of those who will be saved in this dispensation of grace will be reached for Christ during revivals.

The third purpose of a revival — the chief purpose, God help me to tell it, the noblest motive, the highest passion, the only purpose God can really bless, God will bless, God has blessed — is to exalt the Lord Jesus Christ. I am very much afraid that one, if not the chief, reason why God is not blessing our efforts more is that we are selfish, that we have no thought for the glory of the Lord Jesus Christ. That is why many of us are not doing anything. Many of us are not in love with Jesus. We have no compassion for the lost. We work for each other, for our churches, for our pastors, but the least little thing throws us off balance. If we are in love with Jesus, if we have a passion for Jesus, no matter what the difficulty, no matter what anybody else does, our passion for Christ will drive us to give, to pray, to do. We need to exalt Christ. *And I, if I be lifted up from the earth, will draw all men unto me.* Only by enthroning Christ can we claim the promises of God, the fullness of His Holy Spirit, the answers to our prayers.

Consider also the personnel of a revival. Most important, of course, are the Three Persons of the Trinity: God, Christ, the Holy Spirit. There are many things we can do in our own strength. We can visit, advertise, invite, attend services, but, my friends, we are utterly unable to bring about a revival. We need God. We need Christ. We need the Holy Spirit, to convict, to constrain, to convert, to consecrate, to attract. Thank God, I can tell you, dogmatically, positively, assuredly, beyond doubt or peradventure, that the Holy Spirit is eager, longing, able to bless us if we will but give Him the opportunity.

A revival is also composed of church members: Christians — you and I. Give me three hundred people dedicated to God, surrendered to Christ, submitted to the Holy Spirit, who will say, "You can count on me" — give me even two hundred who will go the limit for Jesus, for the Gospel, in the Holy Spirit, for the souls of men — and we will take a city for the Lord Jesus Christ. I have been in campaigns when the people were hot, when the people were cold, when the church was big, when the church was little; I have conducted meetings in the North, East, South, West, from one end of the country to the other. There is, I believe, only one unknown equation in a revival, only one thing that can stop us from having a victory, only one thing that will keep God from giving us a revival. Would you like to know what it is? I will tell you. Look in the mirror. There between the frames of the mirror you will see the only thing that can stop us from having a spiritual upheaval. God is ready, willing, able to bless us. Christ will deny us no good thing. The Spirit's power has never abated.

A revival is also composed of unsaved souls, backsliders, those out of Christ for any reason. If we pray for them, if we go after them, they will come by the scores, by the hundreds. It has been so everywhere. But they will not come unless we go after them. I have heard people say that in olden times sinners came to church. That is not true. It is not in the Bible. The Lord Jesus Christ *went after them.* He sent His disciples after them. It is so in Christian history. It has always been difficult to reach sinners. They have never come of their own free will. The Devil had them, has them, will have them, until we cut them loose by the power of the Spirit from his hold. I believe, I know, with all my soul I am certain, that the unsaved will come to the place of meeting, will come to Christ if and when you and I in compassion, consecration, anxiety, intercession, with yearning, longing, anxious hearts, even weeping eyes, go after them and press the claims of the Lord upon them.

We have considered the purpose and the personnel of a revival. Now let us think about the price of a revival. What is the price of a revival? What did Moses have to pay? What did Samuel have to pay? What did Elijah have to pay? Isaiah? Hezekiah? What price did Joshua have to pay? What price did Peter and Paul and Luther and Wesley and Whitefield and Spurgeon and Moody and Billy Sunday have to pay? Each of us has to pay the same price — exactly the same price. There is no difference. There never will be any difference. God has never changed His terms. Power is costly. The most expensive power in all the world is the power of Pentecost. The price is high — but we can pay it. Here is how.

We must have a personal devotion to the Lord Jesus Christ. If you will study the biographies of these men I mentioned, you will find that they were characterized by one outstanding attitude. They were in love with the Lord Jesus Christ. You and I must fall in love with Jesus. Passion and devotion to Christ will take care of the sin problem in our lives. If we love Jesus we will hate the Devil, hate the world, hate sin. If we really love Jesus, all that might put a shadow between Him and us will be a horrible detestation to us. I wish I could go to each of you, one by one, and ask you, "Do you love Jesus?" I wish I could press the question upon you until your hearts responded with the answer, "Yes, I love Jesus more than I love life itself." We must visit for Jesus' sake. We must invite for Jesus' sake. We must sacrifice for Jesus' sake. We must attend services for Jesus' sake. We must give our money for Jesus' sake. We must preach for Jesus' sake. We must win souls for Jesus' sake. We must have a personal devotion to Jesus — not in word only, but with all our hearts, with all our souls. There must be a passionate devotion that will wake us in the night, that will be with us in the day, that will beset us on every hand, at home and abroad. "Jesus, Jesus, blessed Jesus!" — that must be the cry of our hearts.

The second price of a revival is a purposeful compassion for the souls of men. I say "purposeful" because I mean it. There is compassion and compassion. B. B. Crimm held a revival in Lawton, Oklahoma when I was a soldier at Fort Sill. He could tell fascinating stories about dogs. I went every night I was not on duty. Church members sobbed and wept over his dog tales, but I knew that most of them never prayed, never sought the lost. I do not know what you call that in English, but the Jewish name for it is *hypocrisy*. It is lying. By compassion I do not mean the compassion which causes one to weep when a moving story is told. I mean the compassion that burns high and clear when there is no revival, that flames on Monday even more than on Sunday, and is higher on Tuesday than on Monday. I mean the kind of compassion that gives us no rest nor peace until we give the best of our thought, the best of our talents, the best of our time, the best of our efforts to seeking out the lost for the Saviour. We need a purposeful compassion that will wake us in the morning crying, "O Lord, for Jesus' sake, save our city." We need a compassion that will drive us to our knees and make us say when we go to bed at night, "O Lord, for Christ's sake, save our people." We need a compassion that will seek out and make opportunities to witness for Christ day and night. That is purposeful compassion.

The third price that we must pay for this revival that God wants, that you, Christian reader, want, that I want, is persistent intercession. We must have not only personal devotion to Christ, purposeful compassion for the souls of men, but persistent intercession. We must pray without ceasing. We must pray as we have never prayed before in all our lives. We must pray for ourselves, pray for our fellow church members, pray for the backslidden, the indifferent, the unconcerned, the unconsecrated, pray for the pastors, pray for the evangelists, pray for the choirs and pianists. We must literally saturate our towns with prayers. If I were to ask you the question "Do you believe God answers prayer?" you would answer immediately, "I surely do." Do you? Do you believe God answers prayer? How do you know? Has someone told you? Do you know it "second-hand"? Have you ever tested the truth of the statement? Has God ever answered prayer for you in a mighty, miraculous way? If you believe the Bible is the Word of God, if you believe the promises of God are yea and amen in Christ, if you believe there is a God in heaven, if you believe God can give us a revival, if you want to see a torrential visitation of God's Spirit, I challenge you, I appeal to you, I implore you, I beseech you, from this moment on, without rest or cessation, let us — all of us, each of us — lift our cities to God's throne of grace. Let us keep them there in the white heat of our prayers until God answers by fire and sends us a revival from above.

This is God's plan for a revival. Comply with it and the heavens will flood the earth with showers of blessings. Let us plead God's grace until the Holy Spirit creates within our hearts a burning passion for Christ, a purposeful compassion for souls, a ceaseless intercession for power and victory.

II
THE GREAT CHRISTIAN DUTY

Then opened he their understanding, that they might understand the scriptures, and said unto them, Thus it is written, and thus it behooved Christ to suffer, and to rise from the dead the third day: and that repentance and remission of sins should be preached in his name among all nations, beginning at Jerusalem. And ye are witnesses of these things. And, behold, I send the promise of my Father upon you: but tarry ye in the city of Jerusalem, until ye be endued with power from on high (Luke 24:45-49).

This is the Master's modern message. It is as timely today as when it fell on the ears of the eleven disciples nineteen hundred years ago in old Jerusalem. It has never been improved, excelled or abrogated. We need to meditate upon it, restudy it, measure ourselves and our programs by it, cut out the nonessential, introduce the required.

Here is the scene. Eleven humble men, fresh from their equally humble pursuits, without organization, without exchequer, without social, political, economic, religious standing — eleven men, eleven common run-of-the-mill men — are directed to take over and make over a world. It seems an utterly fantastic impossibility. Yet I say to you that had the succeeding generations of Christians the zeal of those early disciples, the kingdom of God would have come upon earth long ago.

The Great Commission is still in effect, still the burden, the responsibility, the obligation of every Christian everywhere. It is our task to win the world for Christ; to win it, not by powerful states, but by a proclaimed Saviour; not by political systems, but by preaching salvation; not by philosophic schemes, but by personal surrender. This is the work of the Church, the labor of every twice-born child of God.

Consider with me, then, first, the Master's message; second, the Master's messengers; third, the Master's method.

THE MASTER'S MESSAGE

The message is the same because the need is the same. Men are lost in sin, without God, without hope in this world and surely in the world to come. Our minds are attracted and distracted by war, by defense, by complicated problems, but the greatest need of every one of us, and of every other man, woman and child, in America and in all the world, is salvation, redemption, regeneration. Never forget that. Men are lost in sin. They are not going to heaven because they put on uniforms to go out to live or to die for their country. They are not going to escape hell because they buy war bonds or war stamps, because they attend a dance to raise money for the Red Cross. They need Christ, the Cross, the blood, the Gospel. I tell you, it is no longer merely a religious matter. It is our patriotic as well as our religious duty to accept Christ ourselves, to live sanctified, sacrificial, Christian lives, to win others. God, for Jesus' sake, send us a soul-winning revival!

The Gospel is the same. *Moreover, brethren, I declare unto you the gospel which I preached unto you, which also ye have received, and wherein ye stand; by which also ye are saved, if ye keep in memory what I preached unto you, unless ye have believed in vain. For I delivered unto you first of all that which I also received, how that Christ died for our sins according to the Scriptures; and that he was buried, and that he rose again the third day according to the Scriptures* (I Corinthians 15:1-4).

Jesus Christ is the only Saviour. There is no other name under heaven given among men by which we must be saved. There has been and there will be no other revelation from

God, no other way of escape from hell, no other method of
entry into heaven. God help us to disregard all modernistic,
so-called psychological, supposedly scientific vaporings that
would tear the Gospel apart, that would substitute men's
reasonings for God's requirements. Without the shedding
of blood there is no remission. The blood has been shed.
There is balm in Gilead. The Gospel is the same.

The conditions are the same. They have never been
changed. They have never been vitiated, abrogated, repealed.
The Holy Spirit's cry through Paul is the only way out of
sin into salvation: *And the times of this ignorance God
winked at; but now commandeth all men every where to repent: because he hath appointed a day, in the which he will
judge the world in righteousness by that man whom he hath
ordained; whereof he hath given assurance unto all men, in
that he hath raised him from the dead* (Acts 17:30, 31). The
message of first-century preaching is God-honoring and
God-honored — *repentance toward God, and faith toward
our Lord Jesus Christ.*

Preach this same message! Bring men face to face with
the same need. Proclaim the same Gospel. Insist on the
same conditions. The Holy Spirit will do the rest. That is
His business. Crowds will come. Souls will be convicted.
Multitudes will seek Christ for the pardon of their sins.

THE MASTER'S MESSENGERS

The messengers are the same. Every man, woman and
child in all the world who rightfully and righteously claims
Jesus as Christ and Lord is enlisted by the very act and
process of salvation in the ranks of soul-winners. There are
no substitutes, no discharges, no reliefs, no furloughs, no
passes in this campaign. By day and by night, at home and
abroad, in business, in pleasures, the soldiers of the Cross
are to wage unceasing, unending warfare against sin and

Satan for the souls of perishing sinners. Our testimony is
to ring out at all hours, under all conditions, as clear as the
reveille call of a bugler's notes.

My poor heart trembles, my soul grows heavy within me,
my mind is on fire at the thought of what would happen if
one out of five Christian church members of the world would
play fair in this extremely essential yet frightfully neg-
lected business of soul-winning. Think of it: a hundred
soul-winners in a church, five thousand soul-winners in a
city, five hundred thousand in a state, five million in this
nation! Oh, dear God, hasten the day when all this may
come true. Souls — a myriad of souls — would be saved.
Saloons would be closed. Dance halls would be padlocked.
Theaters would go out of business. Churches would be revived. Christ would be glorified, the Devil defeated. Pray,
people of God! Pray with me, blood-washed band — pray
that the Master may make all of us fishers of men.

This is the most practical plan for the Christian conquest
of the world. Mass evangelism, with groups of churches co-
operating in a crusade for Christ and souls, has been blessed
of God. Individual church revivals, with set-apart seasons
for concerted effort to reach the lost and the unaffiliated, are
mighty agencies in the hands of the Spirit. But personal,
hand-to-hand, heart-to-heart, house-to-house visitation and
invitation is the best plan of all, because it is the first plan,
the plan Jesus used, the plan the disciples followed, the plan
that never fails. Ask any spiritual leader in Christ, "What
is the greatest need of our churches today?" The answer
will come without hesitation: "Soul-winners! We need more
soul-winners!"

We cannot all preach. We cannot all teach. We cannot
all sing. We cannot all give great sums of money. Most of
us have but one talent. But we can all pray. We can all wit-

ness. We can all follow Jesus at His behest, that even as He has promised, He may make us fishers of men.

This is the most powerful plan. There is spiritual arithmetic as well as physical arithmetic. If one in God can chase a thousand, if two in the Spirit can put ten thousand to flight, how many more will be overcome, will be garnered in, will be won for the Lord if a hundred of us, if a thousand of us, if ten thousand of us will go out to reap this human, immortal harvest!

Pastor, will you be one? Singer, will you be one? Pianist, will you be one? Choir member, will you be one? Deacon, will you be one? Sunday school superintendent, will you be one? Teacher, will you be one? Circle chairman, will you be one? Usher, will you be one? Church member, Christian, child of God, will you be one?

THE MASTER'S METHOD

The Master's method is the same, absolutely the same, identically the same, without the slightest change the same. It has not, it cannot, it will not, it must not be changed. It is the Master's method. It is the Holy Spirit's method. It is God the Father's method. It is the method of the Old Testament and of the New. It was the method of Moses, of Samuel, of Elijah, of Isaiah. It was the method of Paul, of Wesley, of Moody. It is simple, clear, definite, direct, personal, individual, universal. It is a twofold method. It is, first, to tarry; then, to go.

We must tarry. Patiently, persistently, purposely, we must tarry in prayer at the feet of God. There is absolutely no use doing aught else until we have done just that. Someone has said, "We cannot go farther until we go deeper."

We must tarry before God until the Holy Spirit exposes to us and convicts us of every sin, big or little, in our lives. We must tarry until in humble penitence we have confessed every known and unknown transgression. We must tarry until we know that our iniquities are completely forgiven, that our souls are cleansed in the blood of the Cross.

We must tarry until we see the terrible condition of a lost world, until we see men, women, precious children sinking into eternal hell. We must tarry until our souls are aflame with the compassion that brought Jesus from heaven, that drove Him up and down Palestine, that prostrated Him in Gethsemane, that nailed Him to the Cross.

We must tarry until God gives us a message. Our words are empty, our teachings are futile, our preaching is as tinkling brass and a sounding cymbal unless our thoughts, our reasonings, our dissertations come from God. Unless God sends us we had better not go. Unless the Holy Spirit gives us the word we had better not speak. God has a testimony for every one of His children, but He alone can reveal it to us. We must tarry until the Bible becomes a living, burning, roaring volcano within us, so that we cannot remain silent.

We must tarry for power. Need I stress this? Has not each of you learned the heartbreaking lessons of your own impotence? Have you not fallen dreadfully short of your own standards? Have you not brokenheartedly sought the reason for your own barren fruitlessness? *Not by might, nor by power, but by my spirit,* the Lord is saying to each of us, as He said it through Zechariah to anxious Zerubbabel. Thank God, there is power for us, for each of us, for all of us, power in abundance, power to overflowing.

There is power for every detail, for every venture and adventure of our Christian lives. God is eager to fill us, to thrill us, to inspire and empower us. Let us take hold of God, claim His promises, beseech His mercies, hold on pleadingly until He floods our souls with His almighty Spirit.

After we have tarried — and only after we have tarried —

we must go. In the Name of the Lord, in the power of the Spirit, for the souls of men, we must go. Every one of us must go. The field is white, ripe unto the harvest. We are racing against time, against sin, against Satan, against death. We have no time to waste, no time to lose.

The way will be arduous, the toil heartbreaking. It is a task for courageous, Christ-loving Christians. It will be neither easy nor cheap. The price of souls is great. Jesus knew it on the Cross. We must know it in the field.

Victory is certain. God is on the throne. His promises are yea and amen in Christ. The Holy Spirit is ever with us. Will you take up the challenge, the plea of Christ? Will you be witnesses unto Him — for Him who loved you and gave Himself for you? Will you say to Jesus this hour: "By the agony of Gethsemane's bloody sweat, by the torments of Calvary's rugged Cross, by the burning fires of hell, by the joys and bliss of heaven, Lord Jesus, You may count on me. I'll go!"

III
CHRISTMAS AT EASTER

And the angel answered and said unto the women, Fear not ye: for I know that ye seek Jesus, which was crucified. He is not here: for he is risen, as he said. Come, see the place where the Lord lay. And go quickly, and tell his disciples that he is risen from the dead; and, behold, he goeth before you into Galilee; there shall ye see him: lo, I have told you (Matthew 28:5-7).

There are some who say we ought to discontinue Christmas and Easter. They maintain that these holidays have been devitalized, paganized, commercialized. They point out that bacchanalian orgies of overdressing, overdrinking, overeating have turned these two holidays into blasphemous caricatures of their original meaning and implication. We cannot agree with them. We must have Christmas and Easter. We need them for ourselves. We need them for Christ's sake. We need them for our children's sakes.

We need them for ourselves that we may stop in the mad rush after mundane essentials and nonessentials to meditate again upon the matchless story of the marvelous mercy and grace of God. We need the hushing of our minds, the heartening of our souls, the hope-filling of our lives to be found in the thought of God's great interest in the affairs and activities of a storm-tossed world.

We need these two holy days for our children, that we may pass on to them the fundamentals, the verities, the eternal doctrines of our blessed faith. No amount of teaching and preaching can bring to bear upon a child's heart and mind the old, old story of Jesus, crucified, resurrected, enthroned, with half the effectiveness that a proper observation of these two universal days can give. Christmas and

26

Easter are the heritage of the children of men, to be passed on with loving emphasis, tender regard, careful retelling, from generation to generation.

We need Christmas and Easter for Jesus' sake. It is then that He speaks to us most realistically, most definitely, most dynamically. The awe of the manger, the awfulness of the Cross, the awakening of the Resurrection come to us afresh and anew, stabilizing our faith, inspiring our service, assuring our triumph. Christmas and Easter are bound together with indissoluble bonds. One is impossible without the other. The humble manger precedes the hellish tree. The hateful tree augurs the holy tomb. Had Christ not come in the flesh, had Christ not died on the tree, there would have been no glad Resurrection morning. At Christmas God gave His Son. At Easter God proved Him to be His Son.

It is not enough, however, to theorize about these things. It is not enough merely to think about them or to sing of them. It is not enough to build worship and ceremony around them. They must be known. They must be understood. They must be believed. They must be lived out. May we then, go back to that wondrous morning on which death met his Nemesis, on which the grave was robbed of its sting, on which the hope of a world rests.

The disciples were in a quandary, in fearful doubt, in heart-rending, soul-troubling uncertainty. The Old Testament had not prepared them for any such debacle. They had not understood the meaning of their Master's statements when He had warned them of His approaching dissolution. Jesus was dead — as dead as any other man whose heart the Grim Reaper had stopped. Their half-formed hopes, their bright dreams, their shining anticipations of a glorious kingdom of might and power were gone. They had seen Jesus die. They had seen Him taken from the Cross and buried, a lifeless corpse, in a borrowed tomb. They had seen the great stone seal its entrance. They had seen the Roman guards patroling their beat in front of that stone. This was the end.

After an interminably mournful Sabbath, the women went to the cemetery in much the same fashion as men and women go to the cemetery today, to pay their respects to their beloved dead. There was no thought in their minds of the Resurrection. They did not come to see if Christ had risen. Their amazement was beyond telling when they found the stone rolled away, saw the angelic appearance, heard the message to be delivered to the apostles.

Let us study the message of this angel. First, it speaks of the banishment of fear — *Fear not*. Second, it imparts the inspiration of vision — *Come, see*. Third, it gives us the commission of service — *Go quickly, and tell*.

The angel's message speaks of the banishment of the fear of sin, the presence of sin, the power of sin, the penalty of sin. Sin is still with us. It has crawled its slimy, corroding, corrupting, destroying path through the pages of history and the generations of men. Satan is still on the throne of this world. Temptation still besets us on every hand.

The power of sin is unquestionable and unanswerable. No amount of man's talent, thought, toil, or terms has been able to stem the tide, or stop the encroachments of the myrmidons of hell.

The penalty of sin is still hanging like the sword of Damocles over the heads of the children of men. The fires of the pit have never been banked. The decree of God has never been repealed. The wages of sin is death. The soul that sins dies. Hell is still enlarging its borders to swallow up the unwary, the unfortunate, the unbelieving sinners.

Jesus came into the world to seek and to save these sinners. He came to save His people from their sins. He came to give His life a ransom for many. In the words of Paul,

[*He*] *was delivered for our offences, and was raised again for our justification* (Rom. 4:25). The Resurrection proved to the disciples, and should prove to us, that sin is a defeated enemy, that Satan is a conquered foe.

The Resurrection is, then, the banishment of the fear of death. Death has been the black specter on the horizon of every human life. It is so inevitable, so unavoidable, so inescapable. It takes the young, and it reaps the old. It slays the bad, and it kills the good. It is so mysterious, so uncertain. The grave is so narrow, so cruel; the earth covering our bodies, so clammily heavy. By His Resurrection the Lord Jesus Christ proved that death was not the end of the story, but the beginning — a great, shining, joyous, victorious beginning for those who are in God through our Lord Jesus Christ.

When Jesus said to Martha, *I am the resurrection, and the life; he that believeth in me, though he were dead, yet shall he live: and whosoever liveth and believeth in me shall never die* (John 11:25, 26), it might have been the empty bombast of some mildly mad philosopher, or the vain vaporings of some vapid visionary. But when Christ tore the grave apart to rise from the dead, the Resurrection was a resounding amen to these wonderful words. Because of this, death becomes a relieving experience, a releasing experience, to those who have put their faith in the risen Son of God. Fear is gone. Hope and victory are on the throne.

The Resurrection is the banishment of the fear of the judgment. The Bible is specific. *It is appointed unto men once to die, but after this the judgment* (Heb. 9:27). *For we shall all stand before the judgment seat of Christ* (Rom. 14:10). There is no escape from this dread day, no exception, no excuse. *So that every one of us shall give account of himself to God* (Rom. 14:12). Our sins, transgressions, iniquities and failures are engraved in the archives of glory with a pen of iron in letters of flame. What are we to do? We have no merit to recommend us to the Judge of all the earth. We have no method of approach, of pleading. We have no means of satisfying the just judgment against us. Naked, helpless, hopeless, undone, we stand facing our destiny, our doom.

But, wait, rejoice, give God the grateful praise! Jesus came! Jesus died! Jesus arose! Jesus is on the intercessory throne, at the very right hand of God! We who are Christians, you who will this hour accept Christ as your Saviour, have an advocate, a counselor, a pleading barrister. The Word says so. *We have an advocate with the Father, Jesus Christ the righteous: and he is the propitiation for our sins: and not for ours only, but also for the sins of the whole world* (I John 2:1, 2). The fear of the judgment vanishes; the dread of it is dissipated. The risen Christ, who first died for us, will now represent us, will now speak for us, will now defend us.

The Resurrection is the banishment of the fear of eternity. There is a life beyond the grave, an eternal life, unchangeable, fixed and immutable. Our minds and hearts tell us that there is a hell to shun and a heaven to enjoy. But how? How can we escape the torments of the damned? How can we earn, attain, obtain, retain the joys and bliss of the righteous? Philosophy is silenced. Science cannot help us. Art stands palsied before this eternal problem.

But, thank God, Jesus has an answer. Clear, plain, simple, courageous, inspiring, uplifting are His mighty words: *Let not your heart be troubled: ye believe in God, believe also in me. In my Father's house are many mansions: if it were not so, I would have told you. I go to prepare a place for you. And if I go and prepare a place for you, I will come again, and receive you unto myself; that where I am, there ye may be also* (John 14:1-3).

The Resurrection forever sealed the truth of these tremendous words. God set His seal of approval on them in
the open, empty cave. Easter is a proof, a presage, a promise of the resurrection unto life everlasting of every child of
God. Easter is the title deed to the mansions in heaven.
Easter is the eternal assurance that even our bodies shall
rejoice in the Lord.

Thus the Resurrection banishes the fear of sin by reveal-
ing to us God's acceptance of Christ's atonement. It banishes the fear of death by lifting up before us the one who
tasted death for every man, yet triumphed over this enemy.
It banishes the fear of the judgment by giving us an Advocate with the Father. Finally, it banishes the fear of eternity
by guaranteeing to us our own resurrection and the home
eternal in the skies.

The angel's message also imparts the inspiration of vision.
We need that inspiration. We need that vision. Without
vision we perish in the quagmire of dullness, in the morass
of unreality. *Come, see* is the eternal cry of the angel to
all the ages of men.

Come, see the divinity of Christ. Christ is *declared to be
the Son of God with power, according to the spirit of holiness, by the resurrection from the dead* (Rom. 1:4). The
open tomb authenticates every claim of and concerning
Jesus. In the Christmas story we read that the angel of the
Lord had appeared to Joseph, *saying, Joseph, thou son of
David, fear not to take unto thee Mary thy wife: for that
which is conceived in her is of the Holy Ghost* (Matt. 1:20).
Joseph's empty tomb proved the truth of the angel's declaration. Mary had given birth to the virgin-born Son of God.

Come, see the truth of Christianity. *Moreover, brethren,
I declare unto you the gospel which I preached unto you,
which also ye have received, and wherein ye stand; by which
also ye are saved, if ye keep in memory what I preached*

*unto you, unless ye have believed in vain. For I delivered
unto you first of all that which I also received, how that
Christ died for our sins according to the scriptures* (I Cor.
15:1-3). Other systems of theology have been proposed for
men. Other philosophies of religion have been proclaimed
by men. Other panaceas for sin-sick souls have been propounded to men. This was God's theology, God's religion,
God's revelation, God's cure-all for human ills. The Christmas manger confirmed by Easter morning is proof positive
that God has supplied a Saviour and provided a salvation.

Come, see the power of God. *And what is the exceeding
greatness of his power to us-ward who believe, according to
the working of his mighty power, which he wrought in
Christ, when he raised him from the dead, and set him at his
own right hand in the heavenly places, far above all princi-
pality, and power, and might, and dominion, and every name
that is named, not only in this world, but also in that which
is to come* (Eph. 1:19-21).

In the Old Testament, when the Lord wanted to show a
proof of this almighty power He pointed to the parting of
the Red Sea. That mighty miracle was superseded by this
conquest of death, by this sundering of the rigid walls of
the grave on the Resurrection dawn. No greater demonstration of the omnipotence of God has ever been witnessed
than in the garden by Calvary's hill on that morning. Forever after men could confidently rely upon Him who proved
His ability in such a tremendous fashion as this. *Now unto
him that is able to do exceeding abundantly above all that
we ask or think, according to the power that worketh in us*
(Eph. 3:20) becomes the ringing testimony of all those who
have placed their all, by faith, in Him who raised Jesus from
the dead.

Come, see the hope of man. *But now is Christ risen from
the dead, and become the firstfruits of them that slept. For*

*since by man came death, by man came also the resurrection
of the dead. For as in Adam all die, even so in Christ shall
all be made alive. But every man in his own order: Christ
the firstfruits; afterward they that are Christ's at his coming. Then cometh the end, when he shall have delivered up
the kingdom to God, even the Father; when he shall have
put down all rule and all authority and power. For he must
reign, till he hath put all enemies under his feet. The last
enemy that shall be destroyed is death* (I Cor. 15:20-26).

Here is the guarantee of our justification, the assurance
of the forgiveness of our sins, the hope of the awakening of
the dead, the promise of everlasting life in the mansions of
the blessed. Here is a fact, a historic fact, an attested fact, a
proved fact. Here is something to see, to understand, to believe, to build upon. Here is a way out of sin. Here is a door
out of the grave. Here is an entrance into the grace of God.
Here is a gateway into heaven. Trials may beset us. Troubles
may oppress us. Temptations may distress us. Here is the
hand and the heart of God reaching out to us in the only
begotten, the crucified, the resurrected Son of God. In the
darkest hour, in the most dismal circumstances, in the most
distressing conditions, here is the bright shining hope of
God's love and care.

Let us also consider the commission of service — *Go
quickly, and tell.* The banishment of fear is Christ's part,
leaving His home in heaven, coming down upon the earth,
dying for our sins. The inspiration of vision is God's part,
the raising of Christ from the dead. The commission of
service is our part, the evangelization of a lost world.

Here is a perishing world, men dying in sin, hopelessly
enmeshed in the toils of Satan, powerless, hopeless, helpless.
Here is Bethlehem's manger! Here is Calvary's Cross! Here
is Joseph's empty tomb! Here is the Holy Spirit ready, willing, eager, anxious, able to empower witnesses to the souls

of men. Here is the mighty, hope-giving, life-changing story of a risen Saviour. Consciously, unconsciously, anxiously, listlessly, men are waiting to hear the glad good news. It is ours to proclaim it. It is incumbent upon us to carry on and out this glorious commission.

Tell it! Sing it! Shout it to the ends of the earth! Christ liveth forevermore! Tell the slave of sin that his shackles may be stricken off and shattered from his limbs. Tell the soul in sorrow that a Saviour has had pity on his desperate plight! Point the benighted heathen to the light of the world! Preach to the heartsick idolater the God who lives and breathes, who has power to answer his prayers, to accept his devotions, to recognize his sacrifices and to respond to his worship. Let the sound of it go throughout the earth.

Christmas at Easter makes us debtors to a ruined world. If we believe it, if we receive it, if we rejoice in it, let us, each of us, all of us, prove our gratitude, show our appreciation, display our thankfulness by going out to tell others what the risen Christ means to us.

IV

THE SOUL-WINNER'S PROMISE

He that goeth forth and weepeth, bearing precious seed, shall doubtless come again with rejoicing, bringing his sheaves with him (Psalm
126:6).

This is the soul-winner's text — the simplest, the most
definite in the world. Its directions are positive; its assur-
ances encouraging. God, Christ and the Holy Spirit are
behind it. The testimony of nineteen hundred years supports its assertion. The witness of the great soul-winners
through the ages sustains its direct promise. It is universal,
unqualified, to be accepted and made concrete by all who
have made soul-winning the ultimate aim of their Christian
experience and existence.

Clearly, easily read, on the very face of the verse, are its
three stirring thoughts. The first is the passion of the soul-
winner. The second is the program for the soul-winner.
The third is the promise to the soul-winner. Each one of
these thoughts carries with it a wealth of meaning. May
God help us to understand and carry out these teachings in
our lives.

The passion of the soul-winner is twofold: a burning
passion of love for the blessed Redeemer; a burdening compassion of longing for the souls of men. Who can help loving Jesus? He is so lovely, so loving, so lovable. He first
loved us and wrote out the proof of that love in His own
heart's blood on cruel Calvary's Cross. He has pressed that
matchless love upon each of us in the thousand and one
providential provisions He has made for and in each of our

lives. Yet our love for Him must be nurtured and fed. By communing with Him in the hours of sweet prayer, by studying Him in the pages of the blessed Book, by counting over again the mighty benisons He has bestowed upon us, by looking to the rock whence we were hewn and to the hole of the pit whence we were digged, by contemplating the frightful price He paid for our redemption we grow to love Him more and more. These are salutory exercises. The love for Christ in our souls will wield the power of "an expulsive affection," will serve as a purifying agent in the hands of the Holy Spirit, will give us a weapon against the onslaughts of sin and Satan. Jesus kept sweet in our souls will strengthen us in sorrows, sustain us in toil, supply us with the peace of God which passeth all understanding.

Our passion for Christ will generate within us a compassion for the souls of men. The two are inseparable. They ever go together. Our fellow men are immortal souls whom Jesus loved and for whom He poured out His heart's blood. They may offend us, dishearten us, scold, criticize, even curse us, but for Christ's sake we will love them, pray for them, sacrifice to the limit to reach them with the Word of Life. Christ will take away the sting of their rebuffs, the scorching of their refusals, the shame of their rejections. The knowledge that *the love of Christ constraineth us* will impel us to renewed efforts, inspire us to revived energies, instruct us to redoubled effectiveness. Dry-eyed, dry-hearted, dry-tongued preaching, praying and personal work will never win souls for Christ. Someone has well said, "It takes a broken heart to preach a bleeding Cross." Cry unto God, beloved. Cry unto God for the gift of passion, the gift of tears.

Compassion for souls must be developed, or our work will become matter-of-fact, mechanical. Study what the Word of God says concerning the condition of a soul out of Christ.

Let the awful warnings of the Book burn into your soul. See the doomed and the damned, by the irrevocable decree of God, sinking into the torments of an endless hell. Read the prayers of Moses for his sinful people. Con the tears of Jesus over lost Jerusalem. Hear the heart-cry of Paul as he offered his own great life, as dear to him as our lives are to us, as a ransom for his brethren, his kinsmen according to the flesh. If you are twice born, if you have not backslidden so far that the Holy Spirit cannot break through the armor of your coldness and indifference, of your selfishness and unconcern, these prayers, these tears, these cries will move your hearts, melt your souls, set aflame your minds, constraining you to go afield to win the lost for Christ.

Go into the field. Visit the homes, the business places of all about you. See their bitter disregard of their souls' welfare, their utter thoughtlessness in the matter of their salvation. Think of their fearful blindness in the face of their awful impending doom. These facts and factors will drive you to your knees in sobbing prayer, in burning intercession that the God of infinite mercy may rouse these dead souls to a realization of their awful condition. You will put yourself utterly into the hands of the Holy Spirit that He may use you, all of you, any part of you to rescue these souls from the burning pit of Tophet.

Need I remind you again and anew that without passion there will be no purpose, no power? A passionless Christian is a bitter anomaly. A passionless Christian is the heartache of heaven. A passionless Christian is the laughingstock of hell. God save us from selfish, callous Christianity that takes everything God has to give and renders nothing in return.

> Oh, for a passionate passion for souls,
> Oh, for a pity that yearns;
> Oh, for a love that loves unto death,
> Oh, for a fire that burns!

Oh, for the prayer, prayer that prevails,
That pours out its soul for the lost;
Victorious prayer in the Conqueror's Name,
Oh, for a Pentecost!

Our second thought is the program for the soul-winner.
Let Jesus be our great example in this. Let Paul's life and
pursuits guide us, challenge us, instruct us. What did Jesus
do to win the lost? What did Paul do to rescue the perishing? Two things signalize the lives of both Jesus and
Paul. Intensive prayer was one of them. Extensive witness-
bearing, publicly and from house to house, was the other
element in their success. We can do no better than follow
in their steps. We cannot improve upon their procedure.

We too must heed the admonition of Jesus when *he spake
a parable unto them . . . that men ought always to pray, and
not to faint*. We too must take up the cry of Paul, *praying
always with all prayer and supplication in the Spirit*. If
Paul needed ceaseless prayer, oh, if Jesus required unending supplications, how much — how very much — more do
we. Prayer will condition our lives, leading us to the fountain of spiritual cleansing. Prayer will keep Jesus ever
before us. Prayer will unfold the mysteries of the Word to
us. Prayer will bring the Spirit down upon us. Prayer will
keep us sweet, pure, gentle, yet unswerving in purpose.
Prayer will lead us into the pathway of duty.

Prayer will convict and convert the lost about us. That
doctor of souls, Hudson Taylor, spoke wisely when he said,
"The nearest way to a man's heart is by God's throne of
grace." Conviction and conversion are beyond our scope,
beyond our ability. They are the work of the Holy Spirit.
He and He alone can bring a soul to a realization of its
desperate condition, and to a recognition of its need of the
Lord Jesus Christ. He and He alone can work the miracle
of regeneration in the souls of those whom we are striving
to reach for Christ. Prayer, and I speak reverently, har-

nesses the Holy Spirit to the Word we preach, to our consistent Christian lives, to our testimonies. Prayer multiplies our efforts by the omnipotence of God.

The second part of the soul-winner's program is this: he must go *into all the world, and preach the gospel to every creature.* This Christian generation lacks "going" Christians. We have rich Christians, educated Christians, prominent Christians. We need compassionate, brokenhearted, weeping, agonizing, ceaselessly interceding, "going," witness-bearing Christians. We need Christians who feel a personal, definite, individual responsibility to fulfill the Great Commission.

A "going" Christian will quickly become a glowing Christian, fresh, interested, interesting, studious, attractive, with the dew of heaven and the afflatus of the Spirit upon him. A "going" Christian will be a praying Christian, a loyal-to-the-church Christian, a tithing Christian, a dependable Christian, a victorious Christian.

The Psalmist said it better than I can: *He that goeth forth and weepeth, bearing precious seed.* There is much about which to weep. There is the vastness and ripeness of the harvest field. There is the paucity and scarcity of harvesters. There is our own utter helplessness. There is the soul-destroying unconcern on the part of Christians and the unsaved. There is the race against time, against the hardening influence of sin, against death, against Satan. It is difficult to understand the heart of a Christian who is unmoved, untouched, unbroken at the thought of the perishing multitudes everywhere. What connection there is between tears and power I do not know, but this one thing I can say from experience: I have never seen, and never expect to see, a revival of any magnitude that was not swept in by the weeping agony of God's people.

There is seed to sow. I am aware that much of our witness-bearing is futile because we do not use the proper seed, the Word of God. The average church member has much to say about the size of the church, the excellence of the organization, the graciousness of the pastor, the attractiveness of the program. The very essence of sowing is often left out. There is not a word said about sin and salvation. There is not a word said about the Gospel, the Cross, the blood, the Christ. God has not promised to honor anything save His Word. It is *His Word* that will not return unto Him void. Try it, I beseech you. Give God's program a fair trial. Go into the secret closet to commune with God. Tarry in prayer until you are endued with power from on high. Go out into the harvest field bearing the blessed Word of the Gospel. It will bring forth fruit some thirtyfold, some sixtyfold, some an hundredfold.

Last of all there is the promise to the soul-winner: *Shall doubtless come again with rejoicing, bringing his sheaves with him.* That is the guarantee of God. God's promise has never failed. The "going," weeping, sowing Christian will become the reaping Christian. Jesus said, *Lo, I am with you alway, even unto the end of the world.* Where Jesus goes, there is joy. Where Jesus goes, there is victory. Where Jesus goes, there is fruitfulness.

This promise has never fallen short of fulfillment. Nineteen hundred years bear witness to the fact of the eternal truth of our text. Multiplied myriads of souls now rejoicing in the presence of God, together with the multiplied myriads of the saved still upon this earth, are an inspiring testimony to the verity of God's assurance. Our going, our weeping, our sowing shall not be in vain. All of the power in heaven and earth is at the command of those who do the will of God in this most sacred task to be performed by the children of God.

The joy of the soul-winner is beyond description. It outstrips and outweighs any and every other benediction and pleasure that comes to the human heart. Nothing on earth can compare with it. To know that you have been instrumental in the hands of the Holy Spirit in rescuing a brand from the burning will compensate for every tear, for every toil, for every trial, for every trouble that may come your way in this greatest of all pursuits. To see men, women and children whom you have been able to lead to the Lord Jesus Christ rejoicing in the fullness of salvation and serving God, to meet these persons again and again, to see their smiles of appreciation, hear their words of commendation, — ah, this is a pleasure which the angels covet.

When this life of affliction is ended, when you stand complete in Christ in the presence of God, when you see about the throne the souls who otherwise would have been in the torments of an eternal pit, and hear their voices join with yours in the everlasting song, you will give glory to God for the privilege of being a soul-winner. What shall I say further of the smile of approval of the blessed Lord Himself, of His "thank you," of His *Well done, thou good and faithful servant,* of the crown of reward that the angels shall place upon your head. All these things are awaiting those who give themselves to the task of witness-bearing.

This very day, this very hour, this very moment let us determine in our hearts that we shall be in the ranks of the soul-winners. Let us dedicate ourselves to the task with all that we are and have. Let us count no cost too great, no sacrifice too extensive, no toil too arduous, no task too exacting to accomplish this great duty, God's appointed business. Christ leads the way. We follow in the steps of the apostles. The great of the Church set the pace for us. The Holy Spirit is urging us on. The nodding sheaves of the overripe harvest are beckoning us to the task. From the corridors of heaven, proclaimed by the voices of the holy angels, from the torture torments of hell, heard in the groanings of the damned and the doomed, from the burning needs of the living about us, there comes the cry —

> He that goeth forth and weepeth, bearing precious seed, shall doubtless come again with rejoicing, bringing his sheaves with him.

V
THIS SAME JESUS

And while they looked stedfastly toward heaven as he went up, behold, two men stood by them in white apparel; which also said, Ye men of Galilee, why stand ye gazing up into heaven? this same Jesus, which is taken up from you into heaven, shall so come in like manner as ye have seen him go into heaven (Acts 1:10-11).

Let us study, as the Holy Spirit guides us, these three words: *This same Jesus.* Jesus is the same yesterday, today, forever. I have heard preachers say, but I do not believe it, that in every generation God selects certain men and endues them with power denied to the rest of us. I do not believe that is true, because God would then be a respecter of persons. We can say, however, that there are some men whom God uses more mightily because they make a more definite surrender to the Lord. I believe that each of us preachers can be used just as greatly and effectively in our smaller spheres in the service of the Lord as were Finney, Spurgeon and Moody if we make the same committal to God. Christians today can be used just as fully and mightily in the service of the Lord as were the apostles if they but pay the same price for the same power. Today there are Christians all over the world who are doing apostolic work with apostolic zeal, in apostolic power. Now — not last year, but *now* — in every section of America, Christians and churches are achieving apostolic success, experiencing apostolic victories. As someone has well said, we must not only have the Lord, but, more important, the Lord must have us. If we preachers do not have a hold on our people, if our churches are not active, we ought first to blame ourselves. Ourselves! We do not have the power to draw people and win them. I have had to bite my lips to keep from saying harsh things when I heard people excuse their absence from the Lord's house by declaring that there was too much rain, too much wind, too many Jews, too many Catholics, too many Swedes, too many Modernists. Oh, beloved, there is not too much of anything. There is not enough of the Holy Spirit, not enough power, not enough fire, not enough love, not enough consecration. Oh, brother preacher, oh, deacon, oh, Sunday school teacher, oh, beloved fellow Christian, the channels of our lives are choked and the power of God is not flowing through us. Jesus is knocking at our hearts but the doors to them are shut on the inside. Swing the doors wide open! Let the Lord of Glory enter!

This same Jesus is still the only Saviour. *There is none other name under heaven given among men, whereby we must be saved. This same Jesus* is the only Saviour for a lost soul, and His precious blood is still the only possible agency for salvation. You do not have to explain Jesus. You do not have to apologize for Him. All you have to do is to lift Him up. He will do the rest. It is the same Cross, the same Gospel, the same message. *This same Jesus* is still the only Saviour. Without the slightest hesitation we can still point men to the Lamb of God, still cry, "There is power in the blood, power in the blood!"

This same Jesus still has the same work to do that He started to do, that He commanded His disciples to do, that He wants us to do. This work is to win souls out of sin into salvation, out of darkness into light. Thank God for it. We do not have to ponder, to question, to debate, to investigate what Jesus wants us to do. We have but one task, one work, one engagement, one plan: to preach the Gospel to every creature. All else is secondary. God knows what we need. He sent His only begotten Son to seek and to save the lost. Jesus knows what we need. He sent His disciples to preach repentance and remission of sins in His Name. Again and again He reiterated the task for the Christian, the task for the Church: the making of disciples. How clear it all is, how definite, how powerful, to consecrate and concentrate all our energies in the one driving objective of rescuing the perishing, of caring for the dying, of snatching them in pity from sin and the grave. Oh, if we would but zealously strive to accomplish God's work in God's way.

I am sorely afraid that we are, like Martha, troubled about many things, and forgetful of the most important thing. Christians of today are hard workers; we have more organizations, more conventions, more records, more reports, more standards to reach, more places to go, more things to do than any previous generation. We forget, however, the supreme purpose of our activity. Instead of attacking Satan on the major battleground, we waste our energies and ammunition in unimportant skirmishes. The demons mock our senseless and superficial busyness. Let us restudy Christ's work for us. Let us refuse to be occupied with nonessentials no matter how attractive they may be.

These other things are necessary. I am not minimizing them; but it is altogether possible to pay so much attention to the machinery that the product is forgotten. Machinery is required but, in religious work as perhaps in no other sphere, the less of it, the better. The Holy Spirit will do more to call out, train, organize and empower men and women than all our so-called experts. Concentrate on preaching Christ, on soul-winning, and your Sunday schools will grow, your church attendance will increase, your financial needs will be amply supplied. Your membership will be consecrated. There will be little disturbance. The tides of compassion, of concern, of consecration, of concentration will sweep away grumbling, unrest, disaffection, envy, strife. A soul-winning Christian is a separated Christian. A soul-winning church is a sanctified church, free from the entanglements of a mad world.

Lead your church, your Sunday school, your young people's organization in the one direction of harvesting souls for Christ. Souls saved by Christ will grow, and glow, and go. Keep the needs of souls — perishing and immortal souls — before you constantly. Point them to Christ's compassion, to Paul's passion. Fire them with your own burning anxiety for the hell-bound multitudes. Great will be your reward in the dedication of the saints, in the salvation of the sinners.

This same Jesus still has the same organization ("organism" would perhaps be a better term) through which He has done, is doing, and, at least during this dispensation, will continue to do this same work. There has been no God-permitted change, no Holy Spirit-honored improvement. The Church — the blessed Church — is the evangelizing agency of the Lord Jesus Christ. Some ask, "Which church? What about the different denominations?" My answer is: the New Testament Church, the Scriptural, spiritual, evangelical, evangelistic Church. If you happen to be a member of a body that is neither New Testament nor evangelical nor evangelistic, get out of it and enlist in the ranks of a group that has these earmarks of the Lord.

The Church was built by the Lord Jesus Christ, and its purpose is this: to go to the ends of the earth to make disciples, to baptize them, to teach them to observe all things of the Lord. It is well nigh impossible to be an effective Christian, a fruit-bearing Christian outside of the Church. The Church sent out Paul. The Church, bad as it then was, trained Luther. The Church gave Wesley his start. Moody organized a church. Spurgeon was the pastor of a church.

You cannot be loyal to Christ without being loyal to the Church. You cannot, aye, you will not take your part in and under the Great Commission unless you ally yourself with the Church. Throughout the centuries of Christian history the Church, in the hands of the Holy Spirit, has been Christ's tool for the telling forth of the story of salvation. As you love the Lord, as you are concerned for the souls of men, let your life be dedicated to the building up of the Church catholic, the Church universal.

I pray that God may impress this next thought upon your souls. Not only is *this same Jesus* the same and only Saviour, not only has He the same work for us to do that He started to do long ago, not only does He depend upon the same organization to which we are to attach ourselves in order to do that work, but He also demands of His disciples, of His children, of His servants, of His blood-bought band, of all those who are Christians, the same things He demanded of His apostles, the same things that He has been demanding of all generations of regenerated souls since then. There is no exception, no escape, no excuse. The work is the same. The workers are identical. The procedure is to be the same.

What are the demands of Jesus? Let Him tell you. *If a man love me, he will keep my words.* That is the first requirement. If you are a child of God, born again, washed in the blood, you must show it by keeping His commandments. How are you going to keep His commandments unless you know them? You must therefore spend minutes, hours, days, weeks, months, years studying the Bible. You must know the Word of God. It must throb in your heart, sing in your soul, ring in your mind. You are a citizen of the heavenly Jerusalem. You are a pilgrim on the road to heaven. You are an ambassador for the King of kings. Your conversations both in word and in deed must be savored with the aroma of Canaan. In the Book you will find your road map, your code of ethics, your guide to eternity. No problem can face you but that the Holy Spirit in the pages of this volume will lead you to its happy solution. Let the Bible be your meat by day and your thought by night. Believe it, love it, live it, lift it up to the needs of others all about you.

The first demand of Jesus is that we keep His commandments. The second is this: *Seek ye first the kingdom of God, and his righteousness; and all these things shall be added unto you.* What does that mean? Just this. Give the kingdom of God preference in your home, over your business, over your pleasure. What is the kingdom of God? I do not understand completely and neither does anyone else. I have ideas and opinions. This one thing I do know, that every part of the program of the Church that is Scriptural and spiritual is part of the program of the kingdom of God. We are not seeking the kingdom of God if we are absent from Sunday school, absent from the preaching of the Word, if we do not give of our means to advance missionary interests to the ends of the earth, if we do not ourselves do our best to help win the lost. In seeking the kingdom of God and His righteousness Paul became all things to all men that by all means he might save some. In seeking the kingdom of God and His righteousness David Brainerd toiled out his young life among the savage Indians. In seeking the kingdom of God and His righteousness Adoniram Judson festered his tortured body in Burma's bloody prison. In seeking the kingdom of God and His righteousness we also must count no effort too great, no task too exacting, no expense too costly if it will enhance the glory of the Saviour, if it will discomfit Satan, if it will deliver souls from the pit of hell.

This same Jesus demands, in the third place, that we, each of us, every one of us — men, women and children — go into the harvest field to reap the golden grain of precious souls, to bring the sheaves to His pierced feet. He will use us in this supremely exalted, and greatest of all earthly, perhaps even heavenly, tasks. He will empower us for it. The Holy Spirit will go before us, will go with us, will remain after us to clinch our humble testimonies. In my soul there is a conviction as deep-seated as my faith in God, as my assurance of salvation, namely, that the Lord saves us and lets us live for this one purpose: to witness for Christ and win men for eternal life.

This same Jesus is still the only Saviour. This same Jesus still urges us on to the same work. This same Jesus still uses the same organization. This same Jesus still repeats the same demands. From one end of glorious America to the other, churches, preachers, God's people are meeting the requirements of the Lord Jesus Christ, in His holy Name, by His mighty power winning glorious victories. Men and churches are battering down the gates of hell, giving Satan no quarter. *This same Jesus* is being vindicated in His mighty claims to possess all power in heaven and on earth.

Oh, I beseech you, throw away your alibis. Forget your excuses. Get right with God. Obey the behests of Christ. Meet these three conditions. If you do, you shall see such manifestations of God's grace as will make you and all about you to know that this same Jesus is the same yesterday, today and forever.

VI
CONQUERING PRAYER

And this is the confidence that we have in him, that, if we ask any
thing according to his will, he heareth us: and if we know that he hear
us, whatsoever we ask, we know that we have the petitions that we
desired of him. If any man see his brother sin a sin which is not unto
death, he shall ask, and he shall give him life for them that sin not unto
death. There is a sin unto death: I do not say that he shall pray for it
(I John 5:14-16).

John knew the heart of Jesus. Paul knew the mind of
Jesus. John knew Jesus more intimately than did Paul.
John had seen Him, touched Him, heard Him, watched His
marvelous works of grace and power. Paul was the greater
theologian, but John had more feeling. I owe John the
greater debt, because it was through the reading of John
that I started on the road to becoming a Christian. Someone
said in my hearing, "If you want to know Christianity in a
hurry, read John."

One of our greatest problems is: *Does God answer every
prayer?* If you call "no" an answer, then it is "yes," God
answers every prayer. If you call "wait awhile" an answer,
then it is "yes" again. If you call "get right with God first"
an answer, then it is "yes" once more. Not everything that
we call prayer is prayer. Talking is not praying. I can tell
you without the slightest hesitation, by the authority of
God's Word, that God answers every prayer. There is no
question about it. There are three things involved in real
prayer. Remember, I said *real* prayer. If we really prayed
we should move mountains. These three details are essential.

First, prayer is conditional. Every prayer carries with it
a condition. Your approach to God carries a condition. It is

a threefold condition. First, we must have cleanness of heart. *If I regard iniquity in my heart, the Lord will not hear me.* We must have cleanness of mind, heart, life, purpose and all else that constitutes cleanness in relationship to God, in the sight of God. If there is unconfessed sin in our souls, if we are clinging to some idol, if there is something wrong in our lives, we may talk, but we cannot pray. God will not hear us. We are wasting time and energy. We are insulting God. We are cheapening religion. We are belittling grace. We are presuming on love.

Second, we must have faith. *Without faith it is impossible to please [God], for he that cometh to God must believe that he is, and that he is a rewarder of them that diligently seek him.* Faith is a required condition for prayer. When I first started to preach, I used to think that faith could be obtained by saying, "Day by day in every way I am getting better and better." I thought that if I said often enough, "I am getting more and more faith, I am getting more and more faith," I would eventually have enough faith to move mountains. But this was not so. The more I talked, the less faith I had. One day I read in Romans 10 that faith comes by hearing, and hearing by the Word of God. There are two ways to get more faith: by studying God's Word; by eating the bread of life and exercising the faith which you already have. Both these methods are essential, and both must be practiced. If you gave your children wholesome and nutritious food but did not allow them to exercise, they would become weak and eventually die. They must exercise to grow. The same is true of faith. If you have faith but do not use it, it will not become strong. Read God's Word and your faith will grow. Exercise trust in God's promises and your faith will become robust.

The third condition is obedience. Not only cleanness of life, not only faith, but obedience is essential. *And whatso-*

*ever we ask, we receive of him, because we keep his com-
mandments, and do those things that are pleasing in his sight.*
Even the Lord Jesus Christ when He prayed said, *Not my
will, but thine, be done.* Even the Lord Jesus Christ learned
obedience by suffering. I can say without the slightest
hesitation that obedience is the greatest condition for prayer.
If you get down on your knees and pray, "God, give us
a revival," and are not willing to pay for it with your heart's
blood, you are wasting your time because God will not hear
you. If you say and mean it, "I am willing to pay the price
for a revival," it will come. God will send it. There is no
doubt of it. If your church does not grow, if your Sunday
school does not flourish, if results are tragically dishearten-
ing, there is a reason for it. No one is stretched out on the
altar. There is no passionate, utter submission to God's will,
that He may use you to answer your own prayers. Many
people are not willing to pray because they are not willing
to do the will of God.

Prayer is costly. It costs more than any other practice,
more than any other form of worship. Selfishly, physically,
I would rather preach for two hours than pray for one hour.
When I get down on my knees, when God shows me the
polluted sinner I am, it is not pleasant. That is why many
people will not pray. The Holy Spirit continues to condemn them for their sins; they are not willing to give them
up, and so they will not pray. When you pray with a
burdened soul, when you think of all the backslidden hosts
in our churches, of all of the hundreds and thousands of lost
souls all about you, without God, without Christ; when you
think of how small and weak you are, how very little you
can really do, when you realize how utterly helpless and
dependent you are, your heart almost breaks. You grow
weak with the agony of it.

Prayer costs time. Some people, women especially, say, "I

pray all the time. I pray when I sweep. I pray when I wash dishes. I pray when I care for the children." That's not what the Bible teaches. Jesus said, *When thou prayest, enter into thy closet.* If the President were to come into your home, you would sit down, watch him, listen to him, talk to him. You would not be washing dishes, or cooking, or sweeping, or making beds. Prayer costs time. People excuse themselves from spending much time in prayer by saying that they are not heard for their much speaking. That does not mean that we are not heard for our much praying. This refers to our much babbling, our much repeating. If we are not heard for our much praying, why did Jesus pray all night? Why does the Bible tell us to pray without ceasing? No, prayer is power. Much prayer is much power. Little prayer is little power. No prayer is no power. As a rule, your power will be in proportion to your praying time.

It costs thought also to pray, not only time, but thought. You cannot rush into the presence of God, and present a variety of petitions in a haphazard way. I am interested in China. I am also interested in Africa. I give to missions. I was a foreign mission volunteer when I was in the seminary, but God decided otherwise. My heart is burdened for India, for Brazil, but it is more burdened for the Americans here in our United States, because I am watching them go on in sin, lost, on the road to hell. I would like to see a world-revival. God knows I am doing my best to pay the price for it. But my chief concern is for a revival in our own country, now, during these days. If you are really praying, your heart will lift itself to God in definite, purposeful petition. You will beseech the throne of grace for the one or two things uppermost in your soul. You can tell when a man is really in earnest. His tone of voice, the tenor of his words will tell you clearly enough. When he prays aimlessly, purposelessly, without direction, we may know he has not given much thought to his prayer.

Prayer costs not only time, not only thought, but it costs toil. When you get ready to pray, the telephone will ring, the laundryman will appear, the paper boy will come to collect, the beans will start to burn. There will be all sorts of interruptions, everything the Devil can contrive to put in your way. The Devil is most afraid of you when you are on your knees. Make up your mind that you will pay the price, no matter what the consequences may be. God will let no harm come to you or yours when you are really praying. He will take care of the outcome. Never interrupt your prayer periods. Resist any suggestion of Satan. Wait upon the Lord. Let Him search your heart, try your soul, convict you of your sin, condemn you for your shortcomings, cleanse you, purge you in the white heat of His passion and purpose for you. Prayer may cause you spiritual suffering but it is eminently worth it.

Prayer is not only conditional and costly, but it is conquering. For the past eight years I have gone from one end of this land to the other. I have seen tens of thousands of souls come to Christ in revival after revival. I will tell you why. There is no secret to it. There is nothing to my preaching. There is little to my life. But I believe that God answers prayer, and I strive to practice it. I believe in prayer. Prayer conquers.

It will conquer self. It will conquer sin. It will conquer Satan. The biggest problem I have in all the world is Hyman Appelman. Everything else is trivial alongside of the problems I have with myself. My own soul, my own sins, my own shortcomings, my own lack of faith — these are my biggest obstacles. But, thank God, in prayer I can make Hyman Appelman fit for the use of God. I can study the Bible, and preach, and visit, and still not overcome myself. But on my knees in prayer, the Lord straightens me out. It is the prayer closet that will keep us from being castaways after we have preached to, taught, and served others.

Prayer will conquer circumstances. Lack of talent, lack of training, lack of equipment, lack of help, lack of opportunities — all can be conquered through prayer. Prayer will build your Sunday school. Prayer will fill your auditorium. Prayer will raise your money. Prayer will do everything necessary in the development of the kingdom of God. The power of the churches of any city could be multiplied a thousand times by prayer. We can conquer everything — the world, the flesh, the Devil, all obstacles — by prayer. Prayer is our mightiest asset. Prayer is our mightiest shield. Prayer is the mightiest weapon forged in the arsenals of heaven.

Prayer will not only conquer self, will not only conquer circumstances, but it will conquer sinners. *If any man see his brother sin a sin which is not unto death, let him ask, and he shall give him life for them that sin not unto death.* We can do more to win the lost to the Lord Jesus Christ on our knees in prayer than in any other way. That is the changeless, universal testimony of all soul-winners.

Now there is but one more word, one more question I must press upon your souls. Do you believe that the Bible is the Word of God? Do you believe Jesus meant it when He said, *Ask, and ye shall receive?* Do you believe that God answers prayer? Are you willing to pay the price of prayer?

Let us plead with God in importunate prayer that He may start a conflagration which will sweep like a prairie fire over this entire nation to the ends of the earth. Let us not limit God by our unbelief, by our small concern, by our narrow compassion, by our faltering zeal. Let us claim victory over Satan, for God's Word declares: *Thus saith the Lord, the Holy One of Israel, and his Maker, Ask me of things to come concerning my sons, and concerning the work of my hands command ye me.* God is still on the throne. His promises are still yea and amen in the Lord Jesus Christ. Let us therefore utilize the power of prayer — conquering prayer.

VII
THREE TREMENDOUS TRUTHS

But God commendeth his love toward us, in that, while we were yet sinners, Christ died for us (Romans 5:8).

This is another of the great statements concerning the plan of salvation contained in the Bible. God is very concerned that none of us should miss these eternal truths. You will find these vital verities reiterated in God's Word again and again. God knew that we would be spiritual children all of our days. The best way to teach children is by the process of repetition. The Holy Spirit is the greatest of all pedagogues. His program of instruction follows the psychological principle of stating and restating the facts until they are burned into our very souls.

This text divides itself very clearly into these three tremendous thoughts. First, we are all sinners. Second, God loves each of us. Third, Christ died for all of us.

We are not all Jews. We are not all Gentiles. We are not all of the same nationality, of the same age, of the same sex. We do not all like the same things. But in this one thing we are all alike: we are all sinners.

First, we are all sinners by birth. Over that we have absolutely no control. The Bible says, *Behold, I was shapen in iniquity; and in sin did my mother conceive me.* Again it teaches, *The wicked are estranged from the womb; they go astray as soon as they be born, speaking lies.* This is God's dictum covering every one of us today as it has covered all the generations of men since Adam and Eve. *Can any good thing come out of an evil?* is still the problem of the universe. Because our forbears were evil their wickedness was

reproduced in us. Because we are tainted with sin we pass
on the same corruption to our children. Deny this and you
deny the Word of God, you deny the findings of physiology,
you deny the discoveries of the psychology which is beginning to catch up with the age-old pronouncements of Scripture.

Second, we are all sinners by choice. We all know the
basic requirements of God. We have heard them in our
homes, in our schools, in the pages of the Bible, in our Sunday schools, from our pulpits; we have read them in our
Bibles. Yet, knowing God's will for our lives, we persist in
disregarding it. True, Satan is ever ready, ever present,
ever tempting us; nevertheless, the choice to sin is ours. We
are free moral agents. Irresistibly coerced transgression is
not sin.

Third, we are sinners by conduct. The Bible says, *There
is none righteous, no, not one. If we say that we have no
sin, we deceive ourselves, and the truth is not in us . . . If
we say that we have not sinned, we make him a liar, and his
word is not in us.* We know this by experience. We find no
inherent strength in us to resist temptation. Our minds are
stained with the memories of countless faults and failures.
We know this also by observation. We see others about us,
struggling, stumbling, sorrowing over evil tendencies,
wicked propensities. There are degrees of sinners among
us. We are not all murderers, thieves, liars, but we are all
sinners. We have not all sinned alike, but we have all alike
sinned.

Fourth, we are sinners under condemnation. It is written,
*Behold, all souls are mine; as the soul of the father, so also
the soul of the son is mine: the soul that sinneth, it shall die.*
Again we read, *The wages of sin is death.* That applies to
all of us. *Whosoever was not found written in the book of
life was cast into the lake of fire . . . He that believeth not*

*is condemned already . . . He that believeth not the Son
shall not see life; but the wrath of God abideth on him.*
These are the inexorable, unchangeable, universal decrees of
God. There is no escape from them, no exception, no excuse. We are under doom. The curse of the law hangs over
our heads. We are condemned already. There is nothing we
can do for ourselves, for each other. We are standing on
the brink of hell with the ground crumbling beneath our
feet. We are helpless, hopeless, undone.

But wait! Hearken! There is another word. *God commendeth his love toward us.* God loved us and loves us.
This is our plea. This is our hope. This is our cure. This
is our way of escape. God's love reaches down for our souls!
Oh, the vastness, the wideness, the mightiness of God's love!

It is an ennobling love. Some love is degrading, for
example, the love of Cleopatra, Helen of Troy and Holly-
wood's so-called beauties. There is a love which is nothing
but lust, defiling, debasing, desecrating, dragging down.
God's love is pure, holy, elevating, uplifting. God's love
transforms a sinner into a saint, a slave of Satan into a child
of God. God's love reaches into the very depths of our be-
ings, using the blood of Jesus Christ and the regenerating
influence of the Holy Spirit to cover, to cleanse, to conquer
whatever of evil in stain or tendency there may be found.

God's love is an enabling love. Permit an illustration. In
a Louisiana town, the pastor and his wife had a tiny baby
daughter, Martha, who was learning to walk. One day we
visited the pastor's home and witnessed a delightful scene.
The nurse and the mother were on each side of a room,
Martha between them. First the mother, then the nurse
coaxed the toddler. "Come here, Martha! Come here,
Martha!" The nurse placed her hands underneath Martha's
arms and started her off. As the child took one unsteady
step after another, the nurse gently removed her own hands

from the child's body. Martha hesitated, looked back, then sat down without even trying to walk. Then the mother repeated the process, with the same result. As soon as the child realized that the supporting hands no longer held her, she did not even try to walk. Minute after minute, for a long period, nurse and mother continued the teaching, the loving, the petting, the pleading, until finally Martha assayed a few steps alone.

Oh, beloved, the same is true of God. The only difference is this: God never expects us to walk alone. He never takes His great hands from us. He is a God of infinite, inexhaustible, patient, forbearing, enabling love. What would any of us do without the enabling love of God, keeping us from stumbling, watching over us sleeplessly, tirelessly, eternally, supporting us in trial, sustaining us in sorrow, supplying us in need.

God's love is enduring love. This is not always true of human love. The best of us are changeable, variable, affected by moods and circumstances. We fall in and out of love quickly. The passions of one day become the regrets of another. Oh, how rare on earth is enduring love! Friendships are quickly broken. Misunderstandings are frequent. Time changes us. God's love is God Himself, for God is love, without variableness or shadow of turning. We can depend on the perpetual strength of God's love. We can build on it as on a solid foundation.

The third tremendous truth in this text is that Christ died for us. That was the bitterest condemnation of our sins, the choicest demonstration of God's love. The world may criticize our living. The world may deny our preaching. It cannot disprove the love of God. Given the fact that Jesus is the Son of God, that He lived upon the earth, that He suffered the cruel Roman scourge, that He submitted

Himself to the bitter agony of Calvary's Cross, you, I and all the wide world must believe that God is love.

Jesus Christ died voluntarily. Not all the powers of earth and hell could have forced Him to the Cross had He been unwilling. Of His own free will He bore our sins in His own body on the tree. For sheer, pure, unadulterated love for each of us, He submitted Himself to the torments of hell, voluntarily assuming our nature, our burdens, our sins.

Jesus Christ died vicariously. *He was wounded for our transgressions, he was bruised for our iniquities: the chastisement of our peace was upon him . . . he hath made him to be sin for us, who knew no sin; that we might be made the righteousness of God in him.* It was our punishment that He endured. It was our pain that He suffered. It was our death that He took upon Himself. We live because He died.

Jesus Christ died victoriously. *As it is appointed unto men once to die, but after this the judgment: so Christ was once offered to bear the sins of many; and unto them that look for him shall he appear the second time without sin unto salvation . . . For by one offering he hath perfected for ever them that are sanctified.* By His death this victorious Victim, for all of us, conquered sin, discomfited Satan, defeated death, tore asunder the grave. His victory is ours. Through Him and in Him we are more than conquerors.

What more can I say? I must add a closing thought. We know that we are sinners. Our hearts convict us of that. We know God loves us with an unchanging, unmerited, everlasting love. We know Jesus Christ died for us, spilling His blood to redeem us from sin. God stands before you now. He speaks to your heart. Hear His words. "You are a sinner. You are lost. You cannot save yourself. I love you. My Son died for your sins. There is salvation in His shed blood; in Him is salvation for you. Will you accept the offer of My mercy?"

Oh, beloved, by the burden of sin on your hearts, by the blood of Calvary's Cross, by the mighty love of God, I plead with you. Come to Jesus. He is standing here before you. His pierced hands are stretched out to you, pleading with you to come. If you realize you are a sinner, if you know God loves you, if you realize that Christ died for you, if you have the slightest desire for salvation, accept God's invitation. Take your stand on God's promises — *now.*

VIII
CHRIST'S GREATEST QUESTION

While the Pharisees were gathered together, Jesus asked them, saying, What think ye of Christ? whose son is he? They say unto him, The son of David. He saith unto them, How then doth David in spirit call him Lord, saying, The Lord said unto my Lord, Sit thou on my right hand, till I make thine enemies thy footstool? If David then call him Lord, how is he his son? And no man was able to answer him a word, neither durst any man from that day forth ask him any more questions (Matt. 22:41-44).

I am taking as my text this question: *What think ye of Christ?* It is a question you must face. I am sure you understand that when the Lord Jesus Christ asked it of the Pharisees He knew that they did not believe Him to be the Son of God. One more thing I want you to understand. I am not using this as an excuse or alibi. It is a historic fact. These Pharisees did not have the same proof, the same convincing, convicting certainties which face us, that Jesus is the Christ, the Son of God. All they had was His word and the miracles they had seen Him perform. There were other great Jews who had performed miracles, had even raised the dead, for example, Elijah and Elisha. These Jews could not believe this Man from Nazareth was what He said He was — the Son of God. The Pharisees did not make the right decision. I say without the slightest hesitation, and I say it to the Jews as well as to the Gentiles, that the punishment, the chastisement, the weeping, the pain, the shame of my poor people will never cease until they turn to Jesus, admit their mistake, accept Him as the promised Messiah.

There is no question in all the Bible comparable in importance to this question. All the Bible is written to answer it. There is no problem in all the universe that comes within seeing distance of this problem. There is no quandary that God or man has ever propounded that carries the implications which this query carries. If your answer is right, everything else is right. If your answer is wrong, everything else is wrong. You may have the riches of Croesus, but if you decide against the Lord Jesus Christ, riches will avail you nothing. You may be so educated, so brilliant that your intelligence is beyond equal, but unless you have the right answer to this question your intellectual achievements will not take you to heaven or keep you out of torment. It is more important for you young people to come to a sane, sensible conclusion about this matter than about any of the other myriad decisions you will have to face until God calls you from life to death. I do not know how to present this question to you except by taking God's Word and pressing it upon your hearts.

Isaiah said, *The people that walked in darkness have seen a great light: they that dwell in the land of the shadow of death, upon them hath the light shined . . . For unto us a child is born, unto us a son is given: and the government shall be upon his shoulder: and his name shall be called Wonderful, Counsellor, The mighty God, The everlasting Father, The Prince of Peace. Of the increase of his government and peace there shall be no end, upon the throne of David, and upon his kingdom, to order it, and to establish it with judgment and with justice from henceforth even for ever. The zeal of the Lord of hosts will perform this.*

For unto us a child is born, unto us a son is given: and the government shall be upon his shoulder. That is what Isaiah said about Jesus. But that is not the question. The question is: *What think ye of Christ?*

Back yonder, in the long ago, Jesus turned to His disciples and asked, *Whom do men say that I the Son of man am?* They said, *Some say that thou art John the Baptist; some,*

Elias; and others, Jeremias, or one of the prophets. He said unto them, *But whom say ye that I am?* Peter cried out for all the ages, *Thou art the Christ, the son of the living God.* That is what Peter thought about Jesus. But that is not the question. The question is: *What think YE of Christ?*

In Romans Paul said, *Concerning his Son Jesus Christ our Lord, which was made of the seed of David according to the flesh; and declared to be the Son of God with power, according to the spirit of holiness, by the resurrection from the dead.* Paul also said, *Wherefore God also hath highly exalted him, and given him a name which is above every name: that at the name of Jesus every knee should bow, of things in heaven, and things in earth, and things under the earth; and that every tongue should confess that Jesus Christ is Lord, to the glory of God the Father.* That is what Paul thought of Jesus. But that is not the question. The question is: *What think YE of Christ?*

In Mark we read of this incident in the life of Jesus. *And they came over unto the other side of the sea, into the country of the Gadarenes. And when he was come out of the ship, immediately there met him out of the tombs a man with an unclean spirit, who had his dwelling among the tombs; and no man could bind him, no, not with chains: because that he had been often bound with fetters and chains, and the chains had been plucked asunder by him, and the fetters broken in pieces: neither could any man tame him. And always, night and day, he was in the mountains, and in the tombs, crying, and cutting himself with stones. But when he saw Jesus afar off, he ran and worshipped him, and cried with a loud voice, and said, What have I to do with thee, Jesus, thou Son of the most high God? I adjure thee by God, that thou torment me not. For he said unto him, Come out of the man, thou unclean spirit. And he asked him, What is thy name? And he answered, saying, My name is Legion:*

*for we are many. And he besought him much that he would
not send them away out of the country. Now there was there
nigh unto the mountains a great herd of swine feeding. And
all the devils besought him, saying, Send us into the swine,
that we may enter into them. And forthwith Jesus gave them
leave. And the unclean spirits went out, and entered into
the swine: and the herd ran violently down a steep place into
the sea, (they were about two thousand;) and were choked
in the sea.* The demons proclaimed Jesus to be the Christ,
the Son of God. But that is not the question. The question
is: *What think YE of Christ?*

John said, *In the beginning was the Word, and the Word
was with God, and the Word was God. The same was in the
beginning with God. All things were made by him; and
without him was not any thing made that was made. In him
was life; and the life was the light of men . . . And the
Word was made flesh, and dwelt among us, (and we beheld
his glory, the glory as of the only begotten of the Father),
full of grace and truth.* John, who knew Jesus better than
anyone else, said Jesus was the Son of God. But that is not
the question. The question is: *What think YE of Christ?*

If you were to ask me, "What do you think of Jesus?" I
should say without the least hesitation, "He is the Christ,
the Son of the living God." I believe that Jesus is the Christ,
the Son of God. But that is not the question. The question
is: *What think YE of Christ?*

The very importance of this problem, the very mention of
it, the very responsibility of it, the eternal implications of
it constrain each one of us to examine all the facts in the
case.

First, what think ye of the character of this Man Jesus
who is called Christ? What think ye of His personality?
Of His life? Of His works? He was born under a shadow,
a bar sinister, in a Bethlehem manger. Some people to this

day say He was the illegitimate child of Mary. He was reared in Nazareth, at the crossroads of the world's highways, a wicked city. The town was filled with all sorts of evil, corruption, violence, illiteracy, irreligion. To this day if a Jew wants to insult another Jew he calls him a Galilean. Christ was trained in a carpenter's shop. He had no outstanding scholastic advantages. No college or seminary put its stamp of approval upon Him. At the age of thirty, out of mysterious unrecorded years, He appeared, an itinerant teacher, preaching a new Gospel. Like any other sinner, although He was without sin, He submitted himself to the baptism of John, apparently — apparently, I repeat — unto repentance. The rich ignored Him. The educated ridiculed Him. The high and mighty had nothing to do with Him. There gathered about Him a tiny band of poor, humble, low-caste folk, some of whom were the offscourings of society. He seemed to prefer the company of these outcasts to the society of those more highly respected, of those who could offer Him much more.

Thieves, harlots and publicans composed His court. He went in and out among them, but was untainted, unsullied, unspotted, unstained. For nineteen hundred years His character has withstood the most rigid investigations of both friends and enemies. No man, no ten men, no ten thousand men have been so scrutinized as was and is this Nazarene. Today, almost two millenniums after His sojourn upon earth, no man can truthfully, honestly, honorably, convict Him of the slightest sin of omission or commission. He is more than ever the crystal-clear, the heaven-pure Christ of God. Jew, Gentile, Buddhist, Mohammedan, Taoist, Shintoist, believer, unbeliever—all unite in one eternity-long paean of praise of the superlative Man Jesus. You, from the very depths of full hearts, join that mighty chorus. But you must do more than this. If He was all that artists, poets and philosophers say He was, He is either the only begotten Son of God or the world's chief liar. He declared Himself to be the Son of God. If He is not the Son of God, He is the lowest, the most wicked, the vilest, the most heretical, the most blasphemous, the most impious character who ever breathed. But no one has ever accused Him of being a liar, of telling an untruth. I cannot understand, then, how any unbeliever, be he Jew or be he Gentile, can in one breath say He was the greatest among men, and with the next breath brand Him eternity's topmost impostor. Believe in the unapproachable probity of His character, and you must take the next step and cry, "My Lord and my God."

The second question I want to ask you is: What think ye of His Cross? What think ye, not only of His character, but what think ye also of His Cross? There are some things about his Cross which clamor for our attention. His Cross either proves Him to be the Son of God or declares Him to be the maddest of mad men. First of all it was a voluntary Cross. *Greater love hath no man than this, that a man lay down his life for his friends.* There was once a great merchant vessel that had been shipwrecked. The sailors were forced out to sea in a lifeboat. Their supply of food and water was exhausted. The pangs of hunger and thirst assailed them. As not all could survive, they cast lots to see who would jump overboard and thus conserve the remaining supplies. To jump overboard was, of course, certain death. Two brothers were in that vessel, one single, one married. The married man was to jump overboard. Immediately the brother proposed an alternative. "You have a wife and babies," he said. "I am all alone. I'll take your place." Without waiting for an answer, the youth threw himself overboard, saving his brother's life. That was voluntary, vicarious, substitutionary death. But these men were brothers. I am not belittling the heorism of the act, but they were bound by the ties of consanguinity. Besides, the suffering brother merely shortened his life by a few weeks, or months, or at most years. Eventually the brother would have had to die nevertheless. Jesus was immortal. We were not His brothers. We were not even His friends. We were His enemies, in open rebellion against Him. We utterly disregarded His claims.

Two miners in Kentucky were detailed to blast out some rock. They had a fuse and dynamite sticks. When they lit the fuse a bucket was supposed to carry both of them out of the mine. The dynamite was arranged. The fuse was lit. Both got into the bucket. Through some miscalculation only one man had been left at the top. He could not pull both out at once. One of the miners, a Christian, quickly jumped out of the bucket and pulled the rope as a signal. As his partner, who was not a Christian, went up, the one remaining behind cried to him, "I'm a Christian. If something happens to me, I'm all right." The explosion came before the bucket could be lowered again. Fortunately an overhanging ledge of rock saved the Christian's life. It was a heroic act, but the circumstances differed from those involved in Jesus' death. First, for the remaining miner there was a possibility of rescue. Second, it was merely a matter of anticipating a death that was inevitable. Jesus was born to die. He lived in the shadow of the Cross all His days. He voluntarily took upon Himself the form of a man that He might taste death for every man.

Over in Russia, a nobleman, his wife, his two children, and servant were riding a sleigh pulled by four horses. A pack of ravenous wolves pursued them. The nearest town was miles away. The driver loosed one of the horses. It slowed the murderous beasts as they tore it to pieces, but only for a brief respite. A second horse was loosed to divert the ravening brutes, but in a short time the wolves came on.

No other horse could be spared. The lights of the town appeared, but the wolves were gaining. The servant, turning to his master, released the reins into his hands. With a shouted farewell he jumped from the speeding sled and, drawing his axe from his belt, stood facing the oncoming horde. The fight was not long. The snow became crimson with his spurting blood, but the master, the mistress and the children were saved. The peasant had paid the last full measure of devotion. But he owed it. It was a matter of loyalty and allegiance. He was bound to his lord by a thousand bands of obedience and favors. It was not so with Jesus. He was not our servant, although He made Himself so. He owed us no debt of gratitude.

The Cross was not only a voluntary death; it was also a vicarious death. We die for ourselves. We die for our country. But even then it is for ourselves, for ours, for our own. A mother sacrifices her life for her loved ones, but in this also, it is more or less for self; a father gives his life for the family, but here also the ties of blood are present. It was not so with Jesus. I bid you remember one more thing. When the brother jumped from the boat he became a hero. When the miner stayed behind he became a hero. When the servant gave his life for his master he became a hero. When Jesus stretched Himself out on the tree, the bitterest pain involved was that He was crucified as a criminal. He became sin for us. Think of the agony, of the pain, of the torture, of the fearful shame in that bitter cry, *My God, my God, why hast thou forsaken me?* Dwell in awed sorrow on the eternal pathos of that poignant appeal, *Eli, Eli, lama sabachthani?*

Not only was Jesus' death voluntary and vicarious, not only was the Cross voluntary and vicarious, but thank God, the Cross and the death on the Cross were victorious. The Lord Jesus Christ did not remain in the grave. On the third day He rose again. The Cross was made a symbol of the greatest victory ever won over Satan. The Cross, that implement of torture and shame, became a mighty weapon in the hands of God and of men to tear down the strongholds of sin. *What think ye of Christ?* What think ye of His character? What think ye of His voluntary, vicarious, victorious Cross?

Here is another question for your consideration. What think ye of Christ's conquests? His achievements? Have you heard the story of the Zulu king who came to London and met Queen Victoria, "the White Mother," as the Africans called her? She carried him through the London streets, thrilling him with the display of her superlative treasures. Towards evening they returned to the throne room of the palace. The giant black stood before her, his hands on his spear. Through interpreters he asked her this question: "White Mother, when I go back to my people I will be afraid to tell them the things I have seen. They will not believe these marvels my eyes have beheld. If anybody had told me of them I also would have said they were impossible. I want to take back a message to my country. You are just a woman. Your people are just men, women and children, even as are my people. We have taller, stronger, perhaps even braver men than you have. We have more land. We are a large people. Tell me, what is the secret of your strength, of your power?" Queen Victoria, taking her Bible from the small table beside her throne, rose to her feet. Holding the Book before the Zulu chieftain, she spoke. "This Book, O king, this Book contains in its pages the foundation, the secret, the key to the greatness, the wealth, the power of my people."

Oh, my friends, if only the United States — from the President to the tiniest, dirtiest newsboy — if only all of us would realize that the strength of our nation is Christ and the Bible, what a different story America would have to tell! The Bible is a Book of victory. The Christ is the Lord of victory. His mighty achievements have girdled the globe. His magnificent victories have changed the lives of men, the activities of homes, the affairs of nations, the course of a world.

The conquests of Christ throughout the earth are convincing proofs that He is the Son of God. Scan the pages of history with me. Go back into antiquity. We think of a prince, reared in a king's court, surrounded by all the wealth, ease and luxuries of his time. One day he saw two men struggling, one man scourging another. In hot-tempered haste, snatching the biting lash from the aggressor's hand, he literally beat him to death. For that he had to flee, to give up his princely prerogatives, to hide himself in the desert. There Christ met him, broke him, melted him, molded him, filled him, thrilled him, made him one of the mightiest men this world has ever seen. His name is Moses.

There was another man, a fisherman, as unstable as the stormy waters of the sea in which he fished. He was the original backslider, uncertain, quick to speak and just as quick to repent. Lacking deep faith, venturesome, daring to a fault, he plumbed sin's depths one terrible, never-to-be-forgotten night. Christ met him, broke him, melted him, molded him, filled him, thrilled him, and Simon the denier became Peter the rock, the prince of the apostles.

There was another man, harsh, cruel, bitter, with all the hatred, narrowness and bigotry of a religious fanatic. He was a persecutor of the stamp of Torquemada, and had no patience towards any who dared to disagree with him. Murder was in his heart that day. Christ met him, broke him, melted him, molded him, filled him, thrilled him. Next to Jesus Himself there never lived so great a soul as Paul the apostle. He is the world's foremost demonstration of the divinity of Christ.

Centuries later there was a rowdy man, filthy of language, taking malicious joy in hurting other people, as far away from purity and virtue as sin can lead one. Christ met him, broke him, melted him, molded him, filled him, thrilled him. He became a Christian, a preacher, and faced unflinchingly the arrows of endless persecution. He was jailed for twelve long years. In his cell this Christ-possessed John Bunyan wrote *Pilgrim's Progress*, which is, next to the Bible, the sharpest sword at the throat of the Devil.

There was an alien man, of alien birth, of alien race, trained from childhood to disbelieve the New Testament, to deny Christ, to decry Christianity, without religion, without an ideal of service to his fellow men, with no concern for anything except his own personal welfare and prosperity. Christ met him, broke him, melted him, molded him, filled him, thrilled him, saved him, set his poor heart afire with love. Now he is preaching Christ. My own poor life is an answer to the question *What think ye of Christ?*

Every Christian, every man, woman and child who has bowed low in penitence, in faith, in confession at Calvary's Cross, would gladly, eagerly, joyously shout, *Thou art the Christ, the Son of the living God.*

Now we come to our last thought. We have thought together about Christ's character, about Christ's Cross, about Christ's conquests. Now, my dearly beloved, tell me, nay, tell the angels, tell God, tell Christ, tell the Holy Spirit, tell heaven and earth and hell, what will you do with His claims?

He declares Himself to be the only Saviour. We read, *He that believeth on him is not condemned: but he that believeth not is condemned already, because he hath not be-*

lieved in the name of the only begotten Son of God. He
said, *I am the way, the truth, and the life; no man cometh
unto the Father, but by me.* What will you do with His
claims as Saviour? You know you need a Saviour. You
need forgiveness for your sins. Your transgressions must
be blotted out. You must escape from hell and enter heaven.
Jesus declares that He is the only way. He tells us that He
is the resurrection and the life. You want to be raised from
the dead. You want to be reunited with your loved ones in
glory. You want to sing and rejoice with God forever. There
is only one way. There is only one Name. There is only one
hope. There is only one power. Christ is the way. Jesus is
the Name. The Cross is the hope. The Resurrection is the
power. For nineteen hundred years the claim of Christ as
Saviour has brought men out of sin into salvation; out of
darkness into light; out of death into life; out of despair
into joy; out of defeat into victory.

What will you do with the authority, the ordination, the
appointment of the Lord Jesus Christ as your Judge if you
refuse Him as your Saviour, if, God forbid, you reject Him
as your Saviour? What will you do with Him when you
face Him in the judgment, at the resurrection, at the awful
bar of God? Jesus said, *For the Father judgeth no man, but
hath committed all judgment unto the Son.* To Jesus Christ
has been delegated the awful responsibility of judging the
sins and souls of men. Today, He offers Himself to you as
your Saviour. Neglect Him, refuse Him, reject Him, and
one day you will face Him in all the glory of His awesome
majesty as your stern Judge and inexorable executioner.
You will see your error. You will acknowledge your dreadful blunder. You will seek to undo your fearful mistake,
but, alas, it will be eternally too late. Avoid Him as Saviour
and you will face Him as prosecutor. Accept Him as Saviour
and He will one day welcome you to your reward.

We are again face to face with the burning, inescapable, difference-making, destiny-deciding question: *What think ye of Christ?* Do not evade the question. Do not postpone answering it. Listen to your heart. Let your soul give the reply. Do you believe that Jesus is the Son of God? Do you believe that He died for your sins? Do you believe that God raised Him from the dead? Do you believe that He is at the right hand of God, interceding for you? Do you believe that He has the power, the love, the willingness to save you from your sins, to keep you in His grace, to use you in His service? If you do, there is but one step for you to take. Acknowledge the claims of this Son of God. Accept His Cross. Let His mighty love conquer your heart. Let His wondrous grace transform your life.

You need Christ. Christ offers Himself to you this hour. You will never have a better opportunity, a more auspicious occasion. If your heart and mind echo the testimony of Peter, *Thou art the Christ, the Son of the living God*, let your life support the testimony of your soul. Say it, mean it, believe it, do it, for Jesus' sake.

IX

THE SAVING BLOOD

For the life of the flesh is in the blood: and I have given it to you upon the altar to make an atonement for your souls: for it is the blood that maketh an atonement for the soul (Leviticus 17:11).

That which we have seen and heard declare we unto you, that ye also may have fellowship with us: and truly our fellowship is with the Father, and with his Son Jesus Christ. And these things write we unto you, that your joy may be full. This then is the message which we have heard of him, and declare unto you, that God is light, and in him is no darkness at all. If we say that we have fellowship with him, and walk in darkness, we lie, and do not the truth: but if we walk in the light, as he is in the light, we have fellowship one with another, and the blood of Jesus Christ his Son cleanseth us from all sin. If we say that we have no sin, we deceive ourselves, and the truth is not in us. If we confess our sins, he is faithful and just to forgive us our sins, and to cleanse us from all unrighteousness. If we say that we have not sinned, we make him a liar, and his word is not in us (I John 1:3-10).

My text is found in Leviticus 17:11 and that part of I John 1:7 which reads: *The blood of Jesus Christ his Son cleanseth us from all sin.*

The Old Testament, as you know, is composed of the Law, the Prophets and the Writings. The heart of the Law is the book of Leviticus. The heart of Leviticus is found in the sixteenth and seventeenth chapters, which deal with the Day of Atonement. The heart of these two chapters is the eleventh verse of the seventeenth chapter.

The heart of the Prophets is the book of Isaiah. The heart of Isaiah is the fifty-third chapter. The heart of the fifty-third chapter is the sixth verse: *All we like sheep have gone astray; we have turned every one to his own way; and the Lord hath laid on him the iniquity of us all.*

The New Testament is composed of the Gospels, the Epistles and the book of Revelation. The heart of the

Gospels is John. The heart of John is the third chapter. The heart of the third chapter is the fourteenth, fifteenth and sixteenth verses: *And as Moses lifted up the serpent in the wilderness, even so must the Son of man be lifted up: that whosoever believeth in him should not perish, but have eternal life. For God so loved the world, that he gave his only begotten Son, that whosoever believeth in him should not perish, but have everlasting life.*

The heart of the Epistles is Romans. The heart of Romans is the fifth chapter. The heart of the fifth chapter is the sixth through the eleventh verses: *For when we were yet without strength, in due time Christ died for the ungodly. For scarcely for a righteous man will one die: yet peradventure for a good man some would even dare to die. But God commendeth his love toward us, in that, while we were yet sinners, Christ died for us. Much more then, being now justified by his blood, we shall be saved from wrath through him. For if, when we were enemies, we were reconciled to God by the death of his Son, much more, being reconciled, we shall be saved by his life. And not only so, but we also joy in God through our Lord Jesus Christ, by whom we have now received the atonement.*

So you see, in all this, how the shed blood of the Son of God prevails. The pearls of God's revelation are strung on the thread of Calvary's Cross.

The Bible is a powerless Book and Christianity is just one more religion if these declarations be not the very heart of God reaching out for the souls of men.

The blood doctrine is the basis of the Jewish religion as well as of the Christian belief. The blood is the way of man's approach to God. No one can come before God empty-handed. In the Old Testament the Jews had to have sacrifices, and they had to be blood sacrifices. No Jew could come to God except by and through the blood of some atoning victim.

These atoning victims could be offered only upon a certain altar in certain prescribed ways, governed by definite liturgical regulations. Oceans of blood poured out upon any other altar or in any other place, in any other manner, would avail nothing. God's requirements had to be met.

In the New Testament the requirements are stated even more definitely. Not only can one not come to God except through blood, but it must be one kind of blood: that of the Lord Jesus Christ. Despite the declarations of modernism, we stand or fall by the saving power of the shed blood of the Lord Jesus Christ. If John was right when he said, *The blood of Jesus Christ cleanseth us from all sin,* then Christianity is right. There is hope. There is salvation. If John was wrong, then everything in the New Testament is wrong. The whole system of Christianity rests on the fact that *God so loved the world, that he gave his only begotten Son, that whosoever believeth in him should not perish, but have everlasting life.* If that is true, if the blood is essential, then anything, everything, all things else, as far as salvation is concerned, are not essential, of no avail, of no fundamental help. Here is what I mean. If the blood is required for salvation, then baptism is not enough. If the blood is required for salvation, then right living is not enough.

The ceremonies that men have devised, the organizations that men have established, the schemes that men have proposed, unless based upon and built around and supported by the Word of God, will help no one. At best they are man's vagaries. At worst they are satanic originations imposed by the Devil upon the intellects of men to divert their minds from the essential requirements of God.

Anyone who has ever tried to do personal work has found people who say, "I am all right. I am living right. I am trying to serve God in my own way. I go to church. I live a clean moral life." But if the blood is fundamental — the Word says, *Without shedding of blood is no remission*—then church membership, human righteousness, compliance with creed, are not enough. Only the flowing, cleansing blood of the Lord Jesus Christ will avail. I bid you, therefore, search your heart, examine your soul, see if you are under the blood. See if you have experimentally availed yourself of the Cross of Calvary. Do not tell me you were reared in a Christian home. That is not enough. Do not tell me you have not committed any grievous sins. That is not enough. Do not tell me you were baptized by sprinkling when you were a child. That is not enough. Do not tell me you were immersed. That is not enough. Do not tell me you are living right. That is not enough. Have you been washed in the blood? Are you under the blood? Have you been to Calvary? Have you found for yourself the redeeming grace of God? Do you know beyond doubt, beyond question, beyond peradventure that the blood of Jesus Christ has been applied to your soul?

If there be any doubt, any fear, any question, any uncertainty in your mind concerning this, I beseech you, flee from the wrath to come, accept the offer of God's mercy, confess your sins, profess your faith in the Son of God. Accept Him as your Saviour; enthrone Him as your Lord and Master. Do not, oh, I beseech you, do not be satisfied with anything short of that. Nothing else will stand the fires of the judgment.

There is no more important pronouncement in all the Bible than that contained in the words of my text. If you understand them, if you have availed yourselves of them, it is well with your soul. If you have not, regardless of your condition or origin, your circumstances, anything and everything else about you, you are a lost soul on the road to perdition. May we, therefore, consider this mighty revelation from these three angles: first, the promise of the blood; second, the provision of the blood; third, the power of the blood.

The promise of the blood goes back to the Old Testament, to the very beginning of God's dealings with men. I cannot read you all of the passages, but here are three of them: *And I will put enmity between thee and the woman, and between thy seed and her seed; it shall bruise thy head, and thou shalt bruise his heel.* This foretold the great truth that in God's own good time the Lord Jesus Christ would engage Satan in battle — battle unto the death — that He would suffer terrible pain, but that He would conquer Satan. *Surely he hath borne our griefs, and carried our sorrows: yet we did esteem him stricken, smitten of God, and afflicted. But he was wounded for our transgressions, he was bruised for our iniquities: the chastisement of our peace was upon him; and with his stripes we are healed. All we like sheep have gone astray; we have turned every one to his own way; and the Lord hath laid on him the iniquity of us all.*

The Lord Jesus was our scapegoat. The weight, the woe, the wrath of all of our transgressions crushed Him on the Cross.

In that day there shall be a fountain opened to the house of David and to the inhabitants of Jerusalem for sin and for uncleanness. Surely the fountain that flowed from Immanuel's veins for sin and for uncleanness is not only for Jerusalem and the house of David, but for all mankind.

That fountain, pouring forth its mighty stream of cleansing power, has been for the purging of sin from the souls of men for these nineteen hundred years. It has never abated its flow. It has never lost its effectiveness and efficacy. It is still offered to men as the free gift of God's love.

The promise of the blood is not only given by the prophets in the Old Testament, but is shown in the sacrifices. Every time a Jew offered a bird or a beast at the Tabernacle in Shiloh, or in the Temple in Jerusalem, he pointed to the fact that God Himself would provide a sacrifice for the salvation of a lost world. Every time a priest in the Holy Place poured out blood upon that mighty altar, whose fires burned day and night and whose sacrifices were numbered by the multiplied myriads, the crimson streams proclaimed the eternal promises that God Himself would provide a Lamb whose blood would be available and sufficient for the cleansing of all believing mankind. Not only in the teachings of prophets and in the sacrifices but also in the words of the Lord Himself we have the promise of that cleansing blood. Jesus said, *And as Moses lifted up the serpent in the wilderness, even so must the Son of man be lifted up: That whosoever believeth in him should not perish, but have eternal life. For God so loved the world, that he gave his only begotten Son, that whosoever believeth in him should not perish, but have everlasting life.* Jesus also said, *The son of man came not to be ministered unto, but to minister, and to give his life a ransom for many.* The Lord Jesus Christ further said, *I am the good shepherd, and know my sheep, and am known of mine. As the Father knoweth me, even so know I the Father and I lay down my life for the sheep.*

Thus then, by the Old Testament prophets, by the bleeding sacrifices of the Jewish altars, by the Day of Atonement, by the definite declaration of the blessed Saviour Himself, we are assured that in God's own good time, by God's own good grace, out of God's own good mercy, there would be provided a way of escape from sin. Oh, what joy comes to the heart of the believer, what assurance, what confidence, what definite certainty, what triumphant victory, when he scans the pages of the Bible, reading and rereading the

promises concerning the blood on the altars of the Tabernacle and the Temple.

The second truth is found in the provision of the blood.
Remember this one thing above everything else. Thank God,
from first to last, from beginning to end, in every detail, in
every outline, in every plan, in every revelation, in every
suggestion, in every program, in every requirement, in every
ritual connected with the blood, God was the Initiator, the
Planner. God was the One who described the method of
procedure. Yes, it was God who told Abraham to provide a
sacrifice. It was God who told Moses on the mountain what
sacrifices to make. It was God who ordained the priests,
who were to take in their holy hands the blood the Jews
brought in their unholy hands for the cleansing and purifi-
cation of their souls. I wish I could explain it better than
I am able to do. God said to the Jews, "This is the kind of
atonement and sacrifice I will accept, require and view with
favor. Because of it I will forgive your sins." God provided
it. God prepared it. The steps leading to the altar, the very
stones in the altar, every decoration, every ornament, every
detail of every ordinance, of every service, of every offering
was God-planned, God-revealed. When God said to the Jew,
"If you come and make this kind of sacrifice in this manner
I will accept it," He had to accept the Jew's sacrifice and
forgive the Jew, or break His own promise — a thing un-
thinkable.

This is even more clearly apparent in the New Testament.
Jesus is called the Lamb of God. Surely God provided Him.
He was God's only begotten Son. Mary was merely the
vessel for God's holy seed. Joseph had nothing to do with
Him. The Jews had nothing to do with Him. Of course, the
Gentiles had nothing to do with Him. God gave His own
Son as the propitiatory Lamb. He was a man like you and
me, with all the characteristics of a man — head, hands,

feet, heart, blood, skin, bones, flesh. There was nothing peculiar about his physical manhood. He was just one more Jew walking up and down the length and breadth of Palestine. But if He were only a man, He could not atone for our sins. He could not even atone for His own sins or for the sins of any other one person. You will see that a man — even the best man — could not atone for the sins of the billions who were to occupy the world. But He was not only man. He was God encased in the flesh — God who loved us and took upon Himself our infirm flesh, who clothed Himself with our bodies so that He might taste death for every man.

You ask how I know He is God. You say I take too much for granted. You say, "I will admit He was the greatest man, the best Jew who ever lived, but how can I believe He is God?" Let me tell you. Suppose a woman were to come to you or to me and point to her boy and say that he was her child, born out of the normal human relationship. Would you believe her? Would I believe her? Of course not. Why do we believe that Jesus is the Son of God, God in the flesh? I will tell you why I believe it. You come to me. Show me a man born, as Jesus was, in a stable, reared, as He was, in a carpenter's shop, without scholastic advantages, without social or political prestige, pressed down by the poverty of the lower classes; show me a man who at the age of thirty preached startlingly revolutionary new truths, proclaiming verities greater than all the words of all the other sages combined; show me a man who associated with prostitutes, thieves, gamblers, outcasts, outlaws, drunkards and was never accused of or convicted for a single sin; show me a man who performed the miracles that Jesus performed, who died the death that Jesus died, who was raised out of the grave by the mightiest demonstration of God's power, whose life, teachings and power for nineteen hundred years have

changed the affairs of men and nations; tell me such a man
is God, and I will believe you.

He is God. There is no other explanation for Him. Because He is God He could and did die for our sins on Calvary's Cross. His blood is sufficient for the remission of
every sin of every one of us. If Jesus is God, how much is
He worth? He is worth more than all the rest of the world
put together. His merit makes His death on the Cross
valuable enough, important enough, rich enough, effective
enough to cancel the sins of every one of us.

I have told you about the promise of the blood and the
provision of the blood. There is one more stirring thought
to consider: the power of the blood. How does the death
of Christ nineteen hundred years ago help us today? First,
that blood reconciles us unto God. *God was in Christ,
reconciling the world unto himself, not imputing their tres-
passes unto them; and hath committed unto us the word of
reconciliation . . . For he hath made him to be sin for us,
who knew no sin; that we might be made the righteousness
of God in him . . . For it pleased the Father that in him
should all fulness dwell; and, having made peace through
the blood of his cross, by him to reconcile all things unto
himself; by him, I say, whether they be things in earth, or
things in heaven. And you, that were sometime alienated
and enemies in your mind by wicked works, yet now hath he
reconciled in the body of his flesh through death, to present
you holy and unblameable and unreproveable in his sight.*

If you are not a Christian, you are an enemy of God, an
alien from the commonwealth of Israel, a stranger from the
covenants of promise, having no hope and without God in
the world. Jesus on the Cross has provided a way out — a
way by which you and I may walk freely into the presence
of God. His death moves our hearts, melts our wills, moti-
vates our souls to come unto God by Him. The blood of

Calvary turns our enmity into passionate love and loyalty.

The blood of Jesus not only reconciles us but redeems us. *Forasmuch as ye know that ye were not redeemed with corruptible things, as silver and gold, from your vain conversation received by tradition from your fathers; but with the precious blood of Christ, as of a lamb without blemish and without spot.* We were sold to sin. We were enslaved by Satan. Sentence had been passed upon us. Judgment was levied against us. There was no method or means by which we could escape that judgment, that condemnation, that execution. We were lost, doomed. Hell was enlarging itself to receive us. Jesus came between us and our sins, between us and the curse of the law. On the Cross the sovereignty of God was satisfied. On the Cross the wrath of God sheathed its sword in the heart of the loftiest victim that ever graced an altar. On the Cross Justice and Righteousness, Grace and Mercy met and were wedded in the indissoluble bonds of the plan of redemption.

That blood not only reconciles us, not only redeems us, but, beloved, one of these days that blood will receive us into heaven, into glory. Oh, how many tears of joy and gratitude have I shed over the seventh chapter of Revelation! John was being led through heaven when he came to the great white throne. In front of God were multitudes which no man could number, of every nation, and kindred, and tribe, and tongue, dressed in white robes of righteousness, bearing palm leaves of victory in their hands, singing the praises of God in united, melodious voices. John tells us who they were in these words: *And one of the elders answered, saying unto me, What are these which are arrayed in white robes? and whence came they? And I said unto him, Sir, thou knowest. And he said to me, These are they which came out of great tribulation, and have washed their robes, and made them white in the blood of the Lamb. There-*

fore are they before the throne of God, and serve him day and night in his temple: and he that sitteth on the throne shall dwell among them. They shall hunger no more, neither thirst any more; neither shall the sun light on them, nor any heat. For the Lamb which is in the midst of the throne shall feed them, and shall lead them unto living fountains of waters: and God shall wipe away all tears from their eyes. Our only hope, our only guarantee, our only assurance, our only title, our only password to and into heaven is the blood of the Lord Jesus Christ.

There is one question I must yet ask you: Do you want to be reconciled to God? Are you satisfied with being an enemy of God, a rebel, a criminal with the sentence of the law and the wages of sin hanging over your head? Do you want to be redeemed from your sins? Do you want to be received into heaven when your days on earth are ended? If you do, if you want to be reconciled, if you want to be redeemed, if you want to be received, my friends, I offer you, by every promise in the blessed Book, by every drop of Christ's blood sealing these promises, eternal, unqualified salvation. If you will but accept Jesus Christ as your personal Saviour, if you will but come to God by the Lord Jesus Christ, this very hour your salvation will be assured. There is only one thing for you to do. If you are unsaved, if you have the least desire for God, for Christ, for forgiveness, for heaven, say, "I am trusting Jesus. I want that blood. I accept it by faith." God will surely do the rest.

I invite you, by that dripping blood, by the joys of heaven, by the torments of hell, by life, by death, by judgment, by salvation, to come to Him *now*. Step out on the eternal promises of the Book. Accept the offer of God's mercy. God is waiting for you. Christ Jesus is ready to welcome you. The Holy Spirit earnestly urges you to come. The blood is available for you. Oh, be washed in the blood of the Lamb!

X

THE GREATEST WORD IN THE WORLD

For God so loved the world, that he gave his only begotten Son, that whosoever believeth in him should not perish, but have everlasting life (John 3:16).

It was Martin Luther who called this verse "the Gospel in miniature." Someone else has called it "the Gospel in a nut-shell." Many people say they do not know enough about the Bible to be saved. All you must know to become a Christian is found in this verse. It is the mightiest word God ever spoke to the children of men. It is simple, sufficient, sure. There is no possibility of misunderstanding it, of misinterpreting it. Let us study this verse from these three aspects. The outline is found in the text. First, it speaks of lost sinners — *whosoever believeth . . . shall not perish.* Second, it tells of a lifted Saviour — *God so loved the world, that he gave his only begotten Son.* Third, it promises a lasting salvation — *Whosoever believeth in him should not perish, but have everlasting life.* Let me repeat it. This text speaks of lost sinners, a lifted Saviour, a lasting salvation.

That is all there is to the Bible. That is all there is to Christianity. If these things are true, we have hope. If they are not true, then of all of God's creation we are the most miserable. But, thank God, they are true. When God says, *. . . should not perish,* He describes the condition of all mankind. Every soul out of Christ — young or old, Jew or Gentile, educated or ignorant, rich or poor, without exception, without escape, without excuse — every soul out of Jesus Christ is lost in sin and is on the road to eternal destruction and despair.

If you are not in Christ, you are lost — eternally lost, helplessly lost. You are inevitably, inescapably going to hell. But that is not all. If you are not in Christ, you are lost already. You are lost to God, lost to the Church, lost to yourself, lost to your loved ones, lost to your friends, lost to your business associates, lost in life, lost in death, lost at the judgment, lost through an endless eternity.

When I say you are lost in life I mean just that. God says, *To him that knoweth to do good, and doeth it not, to him it is sin.* Again, *Without faith it is impossible to please [God].* We also read, *He that cometh to God must believe that he is.* You are involved in all these things. You have not exercised faith. You have not come to God. You are not pleasing to Him. The blessings and bounties which God has given you are using for Satan, for sin, for self. Your life is a witness against the Church and not for it. You are a stumbling block in the advance of the kingdom of God. If you are in business, you are lost to your business associates. If you are a soldier, you are lost to your fellow soldiers. If you live at home, you are lost to your loved ones in the home. Why? Instead of pointing them to God and heaven by your own salvation and consecrated Christian living, you are dragging them to the Devil and into hell by your own unbelieving, undedicated disobedience. You are sowing the seed of influence all about you. The thought that should give you pause is this. Eventually you may be saved, you may accept Christ as your personal Saviour, but what about the seed you have sown along the way? There are people all about you; there are people coming after you who will stumble into hell because of your influence. You will face them at the judgment bar of God. Their blood will be on your hands. You will go to heaven; they will go into torment. The seed of unbelief which you are sowing others will reap in a harvest of pain, of penalty, of punishment, of anguish, of agony.

You are lost in death. One day while driving to church I heard a choir singing, "I want to die easy when I die. I want to die easy when I die. I want to die easy when I die." It has been a number of years since I heard that marvelous choir singing that thrilling chorus, but it is still ringing in my ears. Listen to me, men, women, children. Listen, listen! You may not accept my invitation to come to Christ, but you are going to die — and I want to die easy when I die. You may not make a public confession of your faith in Christ, but you are going to die — and I want to die easy when I die. You may not be baptized and join a church, but you are going to die — and I want to die easy when I die. You may never give your life to the Saviour, accepting His precious blood for your salvation, becoming a blessing instead of a curse to your fellow men, but you are going to die — and, thank God, I am going to die easy when I die. I have trusted Christ as my Saviour. I have given Him my life in service.

Picture yourself at the hour of death. The last minutes of life are facing you. They fly past. The death rattle is in your throat. The death dew is on your forehead. Your life's vigor is oozing out of your being. All you can think of is that you have rejected Christ, said "no" to the Gospel, trodden Calvary's blood underfoot. It is a terrible thing to die a lost soul.

You are lost at the judgment, lost throughout an endless eternity. You may escape me; you may never open your Bible, you may resist the Holy Spirit; but when the police officer of God, the death angel, comes for you, you cannot escape him; you cannot deny him; you cannot evade him. It makes no difference where you die. You can have your body cremated and your ashes scattered to the four howling winds of the earth, but the mighty power of God will bring your ashes together, and with body and soul you will stand before the dread judgment tribunal. You will face all the deeds done in the body. You are traveling toward the last assize. Just as sure as there is a God in heaven, just as sure as your mother gave you birth, just as sure as the racing blood pounds in your veins, just as surely will you face God at the judgment. Christians have had their sins judged, punished, pardoned in Calvary's Cross. We, the children of God, have an Advocate with the Father, Jesus Christ the righteous. But not you, if you have not accepted Christ as your Saviour. Unsaved soul, Jesus is not your Advocate, but your Judge. You will face His wrath, not His mercy. You will hear of His doom, not His deliverance. Eternity will record and witness your banishment from His holy presence.

You are lost if you are not in Christ. Whether you belong to a church or not, whether you make a pretense of religion or not, whether you were sprinkled or immersed, whether you were reared in a Christian home or not, unless you have been born again, you are lost. Unless the Spirit of God bears witness with your spirit that you are a child of God, you are lost. If you want to know what it means for a soul to be lost, if you want to know the terrors of the lost condition of a soul out of Christ, you may know it. You may see it. Come with me to Calvary. Stand in the shadow of the Cross. See the King of kings, the Lord of lords, the only begotten Son of God, stretched out on the tree. See the torment, the shame, the heartache, the heartbreak, the blood. Remember that every second of that indescribable agony, every drop of that precious blood is a warning to every lost soul, outside of that Cross, outside of that blood, outside of that atonement, that the wages of sin is death, that the doom of unbelief is hell. Do not dismiss these facts and say that you have enough time. You are lost *now*, and this may be the last time God will open His arms of love to give you the opportunity to escape. You are lost, not by the authority of Hyman Appelman, not by the authority of the Church, but by the unchangeable, irrevocable decree of God's Word, by the authority of God's Book, by the testimony of Christ's bloodstained Cross.

But thanks be unto God, I do not have to stop there. Jesus did not stop there. The mightiest word God ever uttered does not stop there. God sent His Son into the world to provide for each one of us a way of escape, a way out of this lost condition. That provision is the lifted Saviour. *And as Moses lifted up the serpent in the wilderness, even so must the Son of man be lifted up; that whosoever believeth in him should not perish, but have eternal life.* Where was Jesus lifted up? How was Jesus lifted up? The Bible is specific in its statements. First He was lifted on the tree — that bloodstained and cursed tree of Calvary. Paul says, *Christ hath redeemed us from the curse of the law, being made a curse for us: for it is written, Cursed is every one that hangeth on a tree.* Peter says, *Who his own self bare our sins in his own body on the tree.* Hallelujah for Jesus! Hallelujah for the Cross! Glory to God for that tree! If there were no other story in all the Bible, if there were no other message except that bloody Cross, that would be enough to constrain each one of us to come to Jesus, Oh, the torment and the hellishness of that atoning agony! Tell me, what kind of heart do you have that you can reject such love? What kind of blood runs in your veins that you can refuse such grace? How can you look at that tree and turn away from such mercy?

But that is not all. He was lifted out of the tomb. Paul says, *Moreover, brethren, I declare unto you the gospel which I preached unto you, which also ye have received, and wherein ye stand; by which also ye are saved, if ye keep in*

*memory what I preached unto you, unless ye have believed
in vain. For I delivered unto you first of all that which I
also received, how that Christ died for our sins according to
the scriptures; and that he was buried, and that he rose again
the third day according to the scriptures.* Thank God for
the first Easter Day, for that first Resurrection morning.
Joseph's tomb is empty. Jesus did not remain dead. There
was a third day on which the stone was rolled away from
the tomb. There was a glorious, victorious hour in which
Jesus was raised from the dead. Do you believe Jesus Christ
was raised from the dead? Was not that the mightiest
triumph this world has ever seen? Yes and no. There is one
mightier than that. There is an exaltation even greater than
the Resurrection.

Jesus was not only lifted on the tree, not only lifted out
of the tomb, but, thank God, He was lifted to the right hand
of the Father on high. *Wherefore God also hath highly
exalted him, and given him a name which is above every
name: that at the name of Jesus every knee should bow, of
things in heaven, and things in earth, and things under the
earth; and that every tongue should confess that Jesus
Christ is Lord, to the glory of God the Father.* Do you
know what that means? Jesus is at the right hand of God,
vested with all the power, the majesty, the glory, the
authority of time and eternity. Do you know what that
means? It means that God took back His Son unto Himself, embraced Him in His own arms, pressed Him to His
own heart, sat Him down at His own right hand, to show
His eternal acceptance of and satisfaction with His Son's
atoning work. It means that Jesus is on the throne. It
means that this Jesus now offers Himself to you as your
Saviour, and His precious blood for your salvation. You
may depend on Jesus' promises because Jesus is alive, at
the right hand of God. It is enough to make anybody shout

the endless praises of Jehovah. What a message! What a Gospel! What glorious good news!

Today Jesus Christ is being lifted up by the love, the lives, the loyalty of consistent, blood-washed Christians the world over. This humble message, our songs, our prayers, our testimonies, our visitations, our invitations — all are united in the glorious work of lifting Jesus before the judgment-bound hearts and souls of sinners. Oh, believe on Him! Receive Him! Accept Him! Confess Him!

My last word, nay, God's last word in this text is an offer, an appeal, an exhortation. God comes to each of us and says, "You are a sinner, lost, on the road to hell, with no help in yourself. I love you with an everlasting love. I proved it. I sent My Son to die for your sins, to die in your stead. Today if you will believe on My Son, if you will accept My Son as your personal Saviour, I will save you with an everlasting salvation."

Let us consider now the third aspect of our text: a lasting salvation. It is a lasting salvation because the Passion of Christ is lasting. *Neither by the blood of goats and calves, but by his own blood he entered in once into the holy place, having obtained eternal redemption for us. For if the blood of bulls and of goats, and the ashes of an heifer sprinkling the unclean, sanctifieth to the purifying of the flesh: how much more shall the blood of Christ, who through the eternal Spirit offered himself without spot to God, purge your conscience from dead works to serve the living God? . . . And almost all things are by the law purged with blood; and without shedding of blood is no remission. It was therefore necessary that the patterns of things in the heavens should be purified with these; but the heavenly things themselves with better sacrifices than these. For Christ is not entered into the holy place made with hands, which are the figures of the true, but into heaven itself, now to appear in the presence of God for us; nor yet that he should offer himself often, as the high priest entereth into the holy place every year with blood of others; for then must he often have suffered since the foundation of the world; but now once in the end of the world hath he appeared to put away sin by the sacrifice of himself. And as it is appointed unto men once to die, but after this the judgment; so Christ was once offered to bear the sins of many; and unto them that look for him shall he appear the second time without sin unto salvation.* The Passion of Christ on the Cross provided an everlasting atonement, universal, individual, for every sinner, for every sin, for all time and all eternity. God does not require further sacrifice. It was sufficiently, abundantly, satisfactorily, eternally accomplished by Jesus on Calvary's Cross. You need add nothing to it. God requires nothing more from you. It is finished.

This salvation is lasting not only because the Passion of Christ is lasting, but because the promises of the Bible are lasting. *He that heareth my word, and believeth on him that sent me, hath everlasting life, and shall not come into condemnation; but is passed from death unto life . . . All that the Father giveth me shall come to me; and him that cometh to me I will in no wise cast out. For I came down from heaven, not to do mine own will, but the will of him that sent me. And this is the Father's will which hath sent me, that of all which he hath given me I should lose nothing, but should raise it up again at the last day. And this is the will of him that sent me, that every one which seeth the Son, and believeth on him, may have everlasting life: and I will raise him up at the last day.* This promise, not of a preacher, not of a church, but of the Son of God, guarantees that our salvation is lasting. It is a definite promise, and means exactly what it says. It comes from One who has never broken a promise He has given. You may rely upon it fully.

Our salvation is lasting not only because the Passion is lasting, not only because the promise is lasting, but, thank God, because the power behind the Passion, the power behind the promise is also lasting, everlasting. I can make a promise to you and mean it sincerely, but I am a mere man, and a hundred things may force me to break that promise. It is not so with God. His promises originate in omniscience and are supported by omnipotence. Neither time nor eternity, neither circumstances nor conditions can change His mighty authority, His matchless love, His superlative power. The power behind this passion is not man's, but God's. Paul said, *Wherefore he is able also to save them to the uttermost that come unto God by him, seeing he ever liveth to make intercession for them.* Jude said, *Now unto him that is able to keep you from falling, and to present you faultless before the presence of his glory with exceeding joy, to the only wise God our Saviour, be glory and majesty, dominion and power, both now and ever. Amen.* Peter said, *Blessed be the God and Father of our Lord Jesus Christ, which according to his abundant mercy hath begotten us again unto a lively hope by the resurrection of Jesus Christ from the dead, to an inheritance incorruptible, and undefiled, and that fadeth not away, reserved in heaven for you, who are kept by the power of God through faith unto salvation ready to be revealed in the last time.*

What more can I say? You know whether you are a sinner or not. You can fool me. You can fool each other. You cannot fool yourself, and you cannot fool God. You know you are lost if you have never accepted Christ, if you have never taken a public stand for Jesus, if you have never confessed Him before men. I have told you the tremendous truths that Jesus Christ was lifted on the tree, lifted out of the tomb, lifted to the throne. You know that these great facts are true, that the salvation thus obtained is lasting because of the lasting Passion, because of the lasting promises, because of the lasting power. There is one more question to be answered. Here it is. You ask, "Preacher, tell us, what must we do to avail ourselves of this lasting salvation?"

My text will answer this question. *For God so loved the world, that he gave his only begotten Son, that whosoever believeth in him should not perish, but have everlasting life . . . Believe on the Lord Jesus Christ, and thou shalt be saved . . . If thou shalt confess with thy mouth the Lord Jesus, and shalt believe in thine heart that God hath raised him from the dead, thou shalt be saved. For with the heart man believeth unto righteousness; and with the mouth confession is made unto salvation.* If you believe that Jesus is the Son of God, if you believe that He died for your sins, if you believe that God raised Him from the dead, if you believe that He is in heaven interceding for you, if you believe that He can and will save you if you trust Him, that is all God seeks of you. If in the depths of your heart there is a desire for Christ, a yearning for the forgiveness of sins, a longing to be saved, accept Him today. Just as you are, accept and publicly confess Christ as your Saviour. Jesus said, *Whosoever therefore shall confess me before men, him will I confess also before my Father which is in heaven.* Come! Jesus is anxiously waiting for you. Come *now*!

XI
ONCE FOR ALL

For the law having a shadow of good things to come, and not the very image of the things, can never with those sacrifices which they offered year by year continually make the comers thereunto perfect. For then would they not have ceased to be offered? because that the worshippers once purged should have had no more conscience of sins. But in those sacrifices there is a remembrance again made of sins every year. For it is not possible that the blood of bulls and of goats should take away sins. Wherefore when he cometh into the world, he saith, Sacrifice and offering thou wouldest not, but a body hast thou prepared me: in burnt offerings and sacrifices for sin thou hast had no pleasure. Then, said I, Lo, I come (in the volume of the book it is written of me,) to do thy will, O God. Above when he said, Sacrifice and offering and burnt offerings and offering for sin thou wouldest not, neither hadst pleasure therein; which are offered by the law; then said he, Lo, I come to do thy will, O God. He taketh away the first, that he may establish the second. By the which will we are sanctified through the offering of the body of Jesus Christ once for all. And every priest standeth daily ministering and offering oftentimes the same sacrifices, which can never take away sins: but this man, after he had offered one sacrifice for sins for ever, sat down on the right hand of God; from henceforth expecting till his enemies be made his footstool. For by one offering he hath perfected for ever them that are sanctified (Hebrews 10:1-14).

I invite you to study with me Hebrews 10:10, *By the which will we are sanctified through the offering of the body of Jesus Christ once for all.* This text will fill your minds, still your souls, thrill your hearts. *Jesus Christ once for all.* I want you to remember these five blessed words. May the Holy Spirit guide us in our meditation.

First, Jesus Christ is *once for all* in creation, *once for all* in the creation of this entire universe. John said, *All things were made by him; and without him was not any thing made that was made.* When in the beginning God spoke the creating words, they were more than the mere utterance of God. The words were the mighty power of the Son of God bringing the universe into being. But that is not all.

Jesus is also unqualifiedly *once for all* in preservation, in His tender provision for our welfare, for our sustenance, in all the multitudinous providences of our lives. *Whatsoever ye shall ask in my name, that will I do, that the Father may be glorified in the Son* is still the open sesame to the treasures of God. The Name of Jesus gives us the only right we have to go to God in prayer. The Name of Jesus is God's signature on the checks of heaven. Does God answer an unsaved man's prayer? Except for the cry *God be merciful to me a sinner,* He does not. There is only one way to come to God, and that is in the Name of the Lord Jesus Christ. If you do not have that Name in salvation, or if after you are saved you fall into sin and have no right to the merits of that precious Name, your prayers will go unheeded and unanswered. *If I regard iniquity in my heart, the Lord will not hear me,* is still in the Book. It is possible to utter socalled prayers and have them bring a malediction instead of a benediction, a curse instead of a blessing. Unless our hearts are right, unless we come in the Name of the Lord Jesus Christ, our prayers are an insult to God. But even that is not all.

Jesus Christ is *once for all* not only in creation, not only in preservation, but above all, beyond all, over all, in redemption. *In whom we have redemption through his blood, the forgiveness of sins, according to the riches of his grace.* There is no redemption outside the blood of the Lord Jesus Christ.

Jesus Christ is *once for all* in the prophecies, in the types, in the sacrifices, in all of the revelations of the Bible, in all of the manifestations of God to the children of men. Thank God, Jesus Christ is *once for all* yesterday, *once for all* today, *once for all* forever, *once for all* with God, *once for all* with men, and some victorious day, when He chains the adversary forever in the pit of hell, He will be *once for all* with the Devil. In these verses Paul brings us three wondrous truths. They are so superlative that I thank God for the privilege of passing them on to you. My outline is borrowed, but because of its excellence I hasten to bring it to you.

First, Jesus Christ is *once for all* in atonement. *For by one offering he hath perfected for ever them that are sanctified.* He is *once for all* in atonement. *Now once in the end of the world hath he appeared to put away sin by the sacrifice of himself.* He is *once for all* in atonement because of the superiority of the sacrifice, even Himself. You do not need theological training to understand that His atoning body and blood were worth more than the entire universe. The superiority of Jesus over the world He created is so manifestly evident that it needs no amplification, explanation, illustration.

He is *once for all* in atonement not only because of the superiority of the victim, but also because of the virtue of His blood. A person living in the time of the Temple who had committed a sin, brought a sacrifice and the priest placed it on the altar before God. That sacrifice took away the particular sin committed by that person. The virtue of Jesus' blood is for every sin, for every sinner, for all time, for all eternity.

Jesus is *once for all* in atonement not only because of the superiority and the value of His sacrificial blood, not only because of the exceeding virtue of it, but also because of the perpetuity of God's acceptance of the Cross. *For by one offering he hath perfected for ever them that are sanctified.* There is no possibility of falling so far from grace that the superiority, the virtue, the perpetuity of the shed blood of the Lord Jesus Christ loses its power to redeem. Our salvation depends on the tremendous verity that *Jesus Christ once for all* — for all men, for all sin, for all time, for all eternity — made satisfactory propitiation, acceptable to and accepted by God.

The second truth in our text is this: Jesus Christ is *once for all* in enthronement. *But this man, after he had offered one sacrifice for sins for ever, sat down on the right hand of God . . . Wherefore God also hath highly exalted him, and given him a name which is above every name: that at the name of Jesus every knee should bow . . . and that every tongue should confess that Jesus Christ is Lord, to the glory of God the Father.* The enthronement of the Lord Jesus Christ is God's amen to His atonement. God, in raising Jesus from the dead, in taking Him back to Himself in glory, in seating Him at His own right hand, accepted forever His atoning blood as a satisfactory offering for our sins. It was Lockyer who said that the Resurrection is God's receipt for Calvary. If Jesus Christ had died not once but a thousand times, I for one would have doubted His ability to save, doubted the effectiveness of His shed blood had He not been raised from the dead. When God rolled away the stone from the tomb, when Jesus came forth as Conqueror over death and the grave, God, crowning Him with the crowns of the ages, put into His hands all authority in heaven and in earth. Because of this matchless display of power I must accept the atonement of the Lord Jesus Christ as sufficient for my sins. I can have no doubt. If I believe in the Resurrection and Ascension of Jesus Christ, it is easy for me to believe that I am justified by His precious blood. It is easy for me to say amen to Paul when he says, *Being justified by faith, we have peace with God through our Lord Jesus Christ.*

First of all, Jesus Christ is enthroned as King. He is the Lord of lords. Jesus is King. The Bible clearly, unmistakably, eternally, definitely declares, *All power is given unto me in heaven and in earth.* God said to His Son, before Bethlehem's manger, before Calvary's Cross, *Ask of me, and I shall give thee the heathen for thine inheritance, and the uttermost parts of the earth for thy possession.* My friends, that is where we who are the children of God stand. If the Lord has given Jesus the heathen for an inheritance, some day He will come to possess them, to rule over them. If the ends of the earth are the inalienable, eternal inheritance and possession of Jesus Christ by the irrevocable decree of God, rest assured that in God's own good time Immanuel will reign over them. There must be a physical, possessive sovereignty. This text cannot be interpreted in any other way than that Jesus will be enthroned over the affairs of the world.

The term "heathen" refers to the Gentiles. God will give Jesus the Jews. One day God will give His Messiah physical overlordship on the throne of David in Jerusalem, over David's people. The Jews accept that truth, although they deny that Jesus is the Messiah. There is a time coming when Jesus will rule over Germany, over Italy, over Russia, over Japan, over England, over America, over all the nations. All empires, kingdoms, republics and sovereignties will bow before Him, confessing Him to be Lord of all. Thank God! I am hurt in my soul when anything is taken away from His glory. Yet I do not have to be. He can well take care of Himself. He does not need my jealousy. He will work it all out after His own good pleasure, and in His own good time. I believe, as did Job, that I shall see Jesus in my flesh. I am hoping, trusting, praying, waiting, and, in a small way, working for that day. It will be glorious to behold my Redeemer in the panoply of heaven, holding the God-promised scepter of His father David in His mighty right hand, with the nations of the earth bowed at His footstool.

Jesus is enthroned not only as King but also as Priest.

He is a Priest forever, after the order of Melchizedek, without beginning or ending of days, without father or mother. He has already been enthroned as our High Priest, and is in the holy of holies interceding for us. He is not like a man, who can die or sin away his right to be a priest. He is without spot or blemish, without variableness or shadow of turning. He is in the very presence of God. He Himself is the mercy seat. His blood is the atonement He offers as He pleads for us day and night. We all can fully, unhesitatingly subscribe to the statement of Paul when he says, *He is able also to save them to the uttermost that come unto God by him, seeing he ever liveth to make intercession for them.* Jesus Christ is *once for all* in enthronement. God accepted His atonement for our sins, crowning Him with the crowns of eternity, giving Him the power, the prestige, the promise, the position of a high priesthood that shall know no end, of a kingdom that shall outlast time.

You will find one more thing in this text. *From henceforth expecting till his enemies be made his footstool.* Not only is there an atonement, not only is there an enthronement, but, thank God, there is coming a time of dethronement, when the Lord Jesus Christ shall triumph over all His enemies, and we shall be gloriously victorious with Him, in Him, through Him. There are three enemies which the Lord Jesus Christ faces now. We, the children of God, also face them. First, there are the kings of this earth, the dictators, the unbelieving rulers, the godless leaders of men and nations, who are trying to establish a bloody, tyrannical worldly program. Second, there is Satan himself with all his wiles, with all his machinations, with all his cruel power. The third enemy is death.

The first enemy the Lord Jesus Christ will put down at His coming is the kings of this earth, the so-called mighty ones who put themselves above God. *The kingdoms of this world are become the kingdoms of our Lord, and of his Christ, and he shall reign for ever and ever.* What a wonderful world that will be! That is God's answer to Hitler, to Stalin, to Mussolini, to the American Association for the Advancement of Atheism, to all those who try to build a house or a nation without God. There will come a time when in the beauty of holiness, in the acme of power, the Christ of God shall dethrone the lofty ones of the earth.

The second enemy the Lord Jesus Christ will overthrow is Satan. *And the devil that deceived them was cast into the lake of fire and brimstone, where the beast and the false prophet are, and shall be tormented day and night for ever and ever.* Just think of it! There is coming a world without Satan, a world without sin. Would you not like to live in such a world? Thank God, you may, in, and through, and by, the Lord Jesus Christ. Satan seems to be supreme now, but his triumph is short lived, and will soon be replaced by eternal defeat.

The last enemy Jesus will cast down is death. *And death and hell were cast into the lake of fire. This is the second death.* Even death will fall beneath the might and authority of the blessed Son of God. Do you know what that means? Let me summarize it. There is not one of us but has loved ones who have gone down into the grave. The conquest of the Lord Jesus Christ over death means that these dear loved ones in Christ will come with Jesus when He comes. He will tear even their bodies loose from the hold of death. It makes no difference if their bodies were shattered by explosions, buried at sea, pulverized by the passing of the years. Jesus said He would conquer death. He will conquer dissolution. He will bring those who put their faith in Him out of their graves.

I cannot describe our appearance, but I know that our flesh shall be beautified. I will tear the glasses off my face and throw them away to let them sink into hell with the rest of the things that make this world a torment. There will be no more dentists' drills. There will be no more bloodstained operating tables. I believe this earth will be changed and made perfect and beautiful. I am eagerly waiting to see the day when this world will be filled with everything delightful and attractive.

It means one more thing. There will be no more death. There will be no more funerals, no more crepes hanging on doors, no more undertakers, no more mourners, no more funeral sermons. Death will be banished forever by the mighty power of Him who is the Lord of death, but more than that, the Lord of life.

How can we avail ourselves of that atonement, that enthronement, that dethronement? By doing three things. First, we must accept Jesus as our Saviour and His shed blood for our salvation. We must receive His death for our life.

Second, we must give ourselves to Him in service, that we may know we are doing His will, and are well-pleasing in His sight.

Third, by day and night, with singing, with happiness, with rejoicing, with thanksgiving, we must study and meditate upon the Word of God, so that His promises may give us hope, joy, inspiration, assurance. Take these words with you: *Jesus Christ once for all* in atonement, *Jesus Christ once for all* in enthronement, *Jesus Christ once for all* in dethronement, *Jesus Christ once for all* yours forever if you will have Him, if you will accept Him, if you will enthrone Him, if you will live and abide with Him in the blessed pages of His Book, applying its doctrines, obeying its commands, rejoicing in its triumphs. God bless you, each of you, all of you, and save you, and sanctify you, and glorify you, for Jesus Christ's sake.

XII
A GREAT RECOMMENDATION

This is a faithful saying, and worthy of all acceptation, that Christ Jesus came into the world to save sinners; of whom I am chief (I Timothy 1:15).

If a man has received special benefit from a medicine, he will urgently recommend it to others. Paul had experienced the mighty healing, saving grace of the Lord Jesus Christ, the Master Physician of souls. Paul therefore spent his life magnifying this miraculous cure and renewal of his life. Jesus had healed him of guilt and condemnation, of wretchedness and ruin, of narrow bigotry, of bitter zeal without knowledge, giving him in exchange moral and spiritual health, divine communion, Christian usefulness, heavenly hope. Paul was eager for others to know this same Healer, to enjoy this same Balm of Gilead.

Consider with me this great recommendation of the Apostle Paul, which speaks clearly of the Person who came, the purpose for which He came, and the people for whom He came.

The Person who came was Jesus, the only begotten Son of God. The Lord might have sent an angel into the world to save us sinners. He sent angels to Abraham, to rescue Lot, to give Jacob his comforting vision, to outline Joshua's great campaign, to apprise Samson's mother and father of the forthcoming birth of their strong son. The Lord might have sent a man, a great leader, as He sent Moses to deliver the Jews from Egypt, as He delegated Gideon to rescue the Israelites from Midian, as He chose David to discomfit the Philistines. But the Lord caused His own Son to come in the flesh of the virgin's child.

Think of what that meant to God. Think of what He was sending His Son to do; not to build an empire, not to erect a mighty throne, not to govern the populace of some vast province, receiving the worshipful service of teeming multitudes. He sent him to poverty, to loneliness, to sleepless nights, to tormenting days, to self-denial, to suffering, to death. We speak with bated breath of the agony of Jesus Christ, and well we may. We can never overemphasize it. What took place in the Father's soul as He saw heaven emptied of its brightest jewel, as He saw His Son encased in the limitations of a man's garb? Only eternity will reveal what occurred in the heart of God when He saw His Son cruelly lashed, sinfully mocked, rudely crowned, bitterly crucified.

Oh, the very mention of the Father's surrender of His Son for our needs, for our sins, is amply, abundantly, eternally sufficient to give assurance to each one of us of God's unalterable concern and compassion for the souls of men. Here, in this transaction, as in nothing else God has ever done, is the unmistakable demonstration of His love for each of us.

Yes, it was the Son of God who came. In Isaiah 9:2, 6 and 7 we read: *The people that walked in darkness have seen a great light: they that dwell in the land of the shadow of death, upon them hath the light shined. For unto us a child is born, unto us a son is given: and the government shall be upon his shoulder: and his name shall be called Wonderful, Counsellor, The mighty God, The everlasting Father, The Prince of Peace. Of the increase of his government and peace there shall be no end, upon the throne of David, and upon his kingdom, to order it, and to establish it with judgment and with justice from henceforth even for ever. The zeal of the Lord of hosts will perform this.*

Jesus was God — God made manifest in the flesh. From

before the foundations of the world He was in His Father's bosom. The worlds were created by Him. Angels made constant obeisance to Him. His throne was from everlasting, His goings forth from of old. In His hands He held the destinies of creation. The universe breathed, lived, moved at His will.

He was also the Son of Man. In Hebrews 2:9-18 we read:

But we see Jesus, who was made a little lower than the angels for the suffering of death, crowned with glory and honour; that he by the grace of God should taste death for every man. For it became him, for whom are all things, and by whom are all things, in bringing many sons unto glory, to make the captain of their salvation perfect through sufferings. For both he that sanctifieth and they who are sanctified are all of one: for which cause he is not ashamed to call them brethren, saying, I will declare thy name unto my brethren, in the midst of the church will I sing praise unto thee. And again, I will put my trust in him. And again, behold I and the children which God hath given me. Forasmuch then as the children are partakers of flesh and blood, he also himself likewise took part of the same; that through death he might destroy him that had the power of death, that is, the devil; and deliver them who through fear of death were all their lifetime subject to bondage. For verily he took not on him the nature of angels; but he took on him the seed of Abraham. Wherefore in all things it behoved him to be made like unto his brethren, that he might be a merciful and faithful high priest in things pertaining to God, to make reconciliation for the sins of the people. For in that he himself hath suffered being tempted, he is able to succour them that are tempted.

Do you realize the full import of this tremendous assertion? Does it stir your hearts with its fervent truths? Does it kindle a fire of grace and gratitude in your souls? God became flesh and dwelt among us, taking upon Himself all our infirmities. Here is what this glorious fact means to me. If Jesus Christ had been a thousand times the Son of God, if in Him were vested even greater love, mightier authority, weightier glory, had He not, abandoning it all, come to live upon the earth the life of a circumscribed man, He would have been too far above me, too far beyond me. His Person, His power, His heavenly purity would have been merely a source of awe, of fear, even of despair, hardly of love. How could I, a worm, no man, the dust of the earth, look up unafraid into the face of Deity? When I see Jesus, a man, living the life of a man, thinking the thoughts of a man, enduring the temptations of a man, sorrowing the sorrows of a man, undergoing the pains of a man, weeping the tears of a man, dying the death of a man, when I hear Him say, *He that hath seen me hath seen the Father,* my heart grows strangely light within me, my soul is buoyed up, the miasmic fogs of doubt and misgiving are dispelled from my mind. It is a wonderful source of inspiration and encouragement to know that He understands me by personal experience, that He was tempted in all points like as I am, yet without sin. He is not some far-off God on some lofty throne aloof from the fretful cares of mankind. On the other hand, He is personally concerned because of personal experience with the mundane activities of those who live upon the earth.

Consider next the purpose for which He came: to save sinners. He is still in the same business; He still has the same power, the same willingness. Paul's contention, in Hebrews 7:25 — *Wherefore he is able also to save them to the uttermost that come unto God by him, seeing he ever liveth to make intercession for them* — abundantly proves that. Sin is a burden of guilt, a barrier of obstruction, a bondage of slavery of the direst, bitterest sort. Sin carries with it a dreadful penalty. Sin has an appalling power. Sin pollutes by its very presence.

The Lord Jesus Christ saves sinners by assuming their burden, by enduring all the punishment for their sins. This is the purpose of Calvary. Galatians 3:13 says, *Christ hath redeemed us from the curse of the law, being made a curse for us: for it is written, Cursed is every one that hangeth on a tree.* II Corinthians 5:14 declares, *For the love of Christ constraineth us; because we thus judge, that if one died for all, then were all dead.* I Peter 2:24 continues, *Who his own self bare our sins in his own body on the tree that we, being dead to sins, should live unto righteousness: by whose stripes ye were healed.*

This is the finished story of Golgotha. The judgment and the justice of God have found their victims. The wrath of God has sheathed its sword in the heart of the Son of God. The law has been satisfied. The execution has been levied. The awful fine has been paid. Redemption has been procured for all guilty sinners. Nowhere in all the world is there a sin-laden soul whose burden of guilt has not been borne on that tree. Without the slightest sort of hesitation, men may come from everywhere to claim their part in this eternal atonement.

God does not save us and then immediately take us to Himself in glory. We must continue to live; we must continue to strive; we must continue to resist sin and Satan. They are all about us, besetting us on every hand. We have no inherent power to overcome them. The Lord Jesus Christ therefore saves sinners not only by bearing the penalty for sin but by overcoming its indwelling power. This is what Jude meant when he said: *Now unto him that is able to keep you from falling, and to present you faultless before the presence of his glory with exceeding joy, to the only wise*

God our Saviour, be glory and majesty, dominion and power, both now and for ever.

This is what Peter meant when he said (I Peter 1:3-5), *Blessed be the God and Father of our Lord Jesus Christ, which according to his abundant mercy hath begotten us again unto a lively hope by the resurrection of Jesus Christ from the dead, to an inheritance incorruptible, and undefiled, and that fadeth not away, reserved in heaven for you, who are kept by the power of God through faith unto salvation ready to be revealed in the last time.* That is what Paul meant when he said, *Wherefore, my beloved, as you have always obeyed, not as in my presence only, but now much more in my absence, work out your own salvation with fear and trembling. For it is God which worketh in you both to will and to do of his good pleasure.*

Note carefully — very carefully — the words stressed by all three of these writers. Jude says, *Now unto him that is able to keep you from falling.* Peter says, *Who are kept by the power of God.* Paul says, *For it is God which worketh in you.* It is, therefore, God through Christ in the Holy Spirit abiding in our hearts, illuminating our minds, enlightening our souls, empowering our lives, who bestows upon us the grace to resist sin and Satan.

There are many who say, "I should like to be a Christian but I am afraid I cannot hold out." That is undoubtedly the truth. Not one of us in his own strength can resist the evil one. But God can. God is stronger than Satan. Christ is mightier than sin. The Holy Spirit has abundant power for the weakest. You need not hesitate, therefore. Commit your soul unto the Lord in the surrender of faith. Accept Jesus Christ as your personal Saviour, receiving His precious blood for your eternal salvation. Know by personal definite experience the might of the enduring presence of the Holy Spirit. This is the heritage of all God's children.

Were God to save us from our sins then let us live forever, nothing more would be necessary. But even we Christians have a death to die, a judgment to face, an eternity to spend somewhere. The Lord Jesus Christ saves sinners, then, not only by His blood on the Cross, not only by His Holy Spirit in our lives, but also by removing us from the presence of sin, and finally, when He comes again, by perpetually banishing sin from the world. He raises us from the dead. In John 11:25-26 we read: *Jesus said unto her, I am the resurrection and the life; he that believeth in me, though he were dead, yet shall he live: and whosoever liveth and believeth in me shall never die.* He represents us at the judgment bar (I John 2:1-2): *My little children, these things write I unto you, that ye sin not. And if any man sin, we have an advocate with the Father, Jesus Christ the righteous: and he is the propitiation for our sins: and not for our's only, but also for the sins of the whole world.* He takes us to Himself in glory (John 14:1-2-3): *Let not your heart be troubled: ye believe in God, believe also in me. In my Father's house are many mansions: if it were not so, I would have told you. I go to prepare a place for you. And if I go and prepare a place for you, I will come again, and receive you unto myself, that where I am, there ye may be also.*

What a wonderful description the Word gives us of the redeemed hosts in glory! How the heart of the Apostle John must have thrilled when he had the glorious experience recorded in Revelation 7:9-17: *After this I beheld, and, lo, a great multitude, which no man could number, of all nations, and kindreds, and people, and tongues, stood before the throne, and before the Lamb, clothed with white robes, and palms in their hands; and cried with a loud voice, saying, Salvation to our God which sitteth upon the throne, and unto the Lamb. And all the angels stood round about the*

throne, and about the elders and the four beasts, and fell be-
fore the throne on their faces, and worshipped God, saying,
Amen: Blessing, and glory, and wisdom, and thanksgiving,
and honour, and power, and might, be unto our God for ever
and ever, Amen. And one of the elders answered, saying
unto me, What are these which are arrayed in white robes?
and whence came they? And I said unto him, Sir, thou
knowest. And he said to me, These are they which came out
of great tribulation, and have washed their robes, and made
them white in the blood of the Lamb. Therefore are they be-
fore the throne of God, and serve him day and night in his
temple; and he that sitteth on the throne shall dwell among
them. They shall hunger no more, neither thirst any more;
neither shall the sun light on them, nor any heat. For the
Lamb which is in the midst of the throne shall feed them,
and shall lead them unto living fountains of waters: and
God shall wipe away all tears from their eyes.

Thus you see the wondrous finished work of the Lord
Jesus Christ for and in every one of us contained in the
blessed words of our text: . . . *that Christ Jesus came into*
the world to save sinners. Provision is made for both the
past and the present. The future is as bright as the promises
and the compassion of God. There is nothing omitted. There
is nothing wanting. Every problem, every exigency has
been anticipated. God's plan of redemption is perfect.

Consider last of all the people for whom Jesus came:
sinners. The word is specific. It is "sinners." Jesus said,
They that be whole need not a physician, but they that are
sick . . . I am not come to call the righteous, but sinners to
repentance. There is a marvelous story told concerning an
experience in the life of that great saint Lady Huntington.
On one of her visits to an English penitentiary she came to
the cell of a deeply despondent man. She did not know it,
but he happened to be the brother of George Whitefield, the

great preacher. Mrs. Huntington could not cheer him. She asked the cause of his discouragement.

"Lady," he said, "I am in dreadful sin."

"Thank God," she said.

"I am the worst sinner in the world," the man groaned.

"Thank God," she replied once more.

The man looked at her, startled.

"I thought you were a Christian," he said. "How can you mock me by thanking God when I tell you that I am the worst sinner in all the world?"

Lady Huntington opened her Bible to the text we are considering and quietly read, *This is a faithful saying, and worthy of all acceptation, that Christ Jesus came into the world to save sinners; of whom I am chief.*

"That is why I am thanking God. Jesus came to save the chief of sinners. There is abundant hope for you."

Right then and there, in that miserable jail cell, the guilty man made his surrender to the Lord Jesus Christ, receiving in exchange for his bitter sins the eternal salvation which was his in Christ. You also may have the same salvation. You also may know that your sins are forgiven. You also may feel the coursing power of the indwelling Holy Spirit. You also may have the assurance of life everlasting, the home eternal in the heavens. If you know yourself to be a sinner, if you know that Christ Jesus came into the world to save sinners, if this very hour you are willing to submit to His power by entrusting your soul and yourself to His eternal mercies, the arms of grace are wide open. Come and welcome. Step out on this glorious assurance. You also will thereafter and forever be able to say, *This is a faithful saying, and worthy of all acceptation, that Christ Jesus came into the world to save sinners; of whom I am chief.*

XIII
GREAT AND PRECIOUS PROMISES

Simon Peter, a servant and an apostle of Jesus Christ, to them that
have obtained like precious faith with us through the righteousness of
God and our Saviour Jesus Christ: grace and peace be multiplied unto
you through the knowledge of God, and of Jesus our Lord, according as
his divine power hath given unto us all things that pertain unto life and
godliness, through the knowledge of him that hath called us to glory
and virtue: whereby are given unto us exceeding great and precious
promises: that by these ye might be partakers of the divine nature, having escaped the corruption that is in the world through lust (II Peter
1:1-4).

Consider with me the encouraging thought of the exceeding great and precious promises of God. There are no truer,
and sweeter statements in the Bible than those found in the
exceeding great and precious promises.

Some people have a strange conception of faith. Faith is
the direct opposite of feeling. If you have faith you must
not depend on feeling. If you have feeling you still need
faith. Feeling changes. Faith does not. The Bible's greatest statement regarding faith is not *Faith is the substance of
things hoped for, the evidence of things not seen*. I can cite
two which are better than that. At least they seem clearer
to me. Here is the first: *But these are written, that ye might
believe that Jesus is the Christ, the Son of God; and that
believing ye might have life through his name*. The second
is this: *So then faith cometh by hearing, and hearing by the
word of God*. The unalterable, unchangeable, eternal Word
of God is the source, the substance, the sum of my faith.

If you were to ask me, "Are you saved?" I would answer
at once, "Yes." If you were to ask me, "How do you know
you are saved?" I should not say, "Because I feel it." Sometimes I do feel it and sometimes I do not. I know I am

saved because God says so, because the Bible says so, because I have done what God told me to do in His Word, because I have done what God required me to do in His revelation, and I know God will do what He said He would do. His Word is unchangeable, and abideth the same forever. My faith is not based on anything in myself. It is based entirely on something altogether outside of myself. There is nothing in me, never was, and never will be, on which to build any sort of faith, even the slightest. I have absolutely no hope in Hyman Appelman, no confidence, no trust in him. I tell you I do not have any more faith in Hyman Appelman than I have in the Devil. But I do have faith in Hyman Appelman's Jesus, in Hyman Appelman's Bible. The foundation for this statement, *The exceeding great and precious promises,* is found in God's Book, God's Word, God's honor.

What makes those promises so *exceeding great and precious?* First, there is their source. They are promises made by God, not by man nor by some organization or group of men, but by God. I may make a promise to you and fully intend to keep it. Some hindrance may arise. I may become ill or die or lose my ability to perform the deed involved, and thus my honestly intended promise may be broken. It is no fault of mine. I had intended to fulfill it. But I am a man, and circumstances may compel me to break my word. Can you think of any conditions which make it impossible for God to keep His promises? I may make a promise to you, believing in you, in your truthfulness, in your probity. You may be a swindler trying to take advantage of me. I may discover this and find I cannot keep my promise to you. But God knows all about you. You cannot fool God. You cannot mislead God. He makes us promises knowing in advance everything about us, our sins and shortcomings, all that may happen — and the moment we

comply with the conditions in His offer, He will keep faith
with us. God is behind His promises. His authority, His
immortality, His unchangeableness, His invariableness, His
majesty, His power, His honor — all are involved in His
pledged word. These promises are exceeding great and
precious because they come from almighty God who can
perform them under any circumstance, under all conditions,
because He knew these circumstances and conditions long
before they appeared, long before He made those promises.
Nothing can surprise him, or intimidate Him, or render Him
impotent. Nothing can alter Him from the course He set
out for Himself from before the beginning of time.

God's promises are *exceeding great and precious*, in the
second place, because of their scope, the area they cover.
They are great not only because of their source but because
of their scope. What do you need? Food? Shelter?
Clothing? A roof over your head? A job at which to earn
your daily bread? God says to you, *Ask, and it shall be
given you; seek, and ye shall find; knock, and it shall be
opened unto you: for every one that asketh receiveth; and
he that seeketh findeth; and to him that knocketh it shall be
opened. Or what man is there of you, whom if his son ask
bread, will he give him a stone? Or if he ask a fish, will he
give him a serpent? If ye then, being evil, know how to give
good gifts unto your children, how much more shall your
Father which is in heaven give good things to them that ask
him?* Paul said at the end of his life, *My God shall supply
all your need according to his riches in glory by Christ
Jesus*. Paul put God to the test in every conceivable way.

What do you need? Salvation? Forgiveness of your
sins? Adoption into the family of God? God says to you,
*Whosoever shall call upon the name of the Lord shall be
saved . . . If thou shalt confess with thy mouth the Lord
Jesus Christ, and shalt believe in thine heart that God hath*

raised him from the dead, thou shalt be saved. What do you need? You need wisdom. Oh, how you need wisdom in this day when all sorts of suggestions, all sorts of voices, all sorts of philosophies, all sorts of schemes beset you and cry from every page, from every platform, from every radio.

"You ought to learn how to drink properly. You ought to learn how to smoke properly. You ought to learn how to dance properly. If you wear the proper arch supports you will be President of the United States." True, I exaggerate, but read current advertisements, listen to the vaporings of the so-called modern philosophers. See if you are not lost in a maze of foolish speculations. God's Word is clear: *If any of you lack wisdom, let him ask of God, that giveth to all men liberally, and upbraideth not; and it shall be given him.* He will tell us which of the many voices to hear and heed. He will tell us in which of the many programs to engage for the glory of the Lord and for our own eternal welfare.

What do you need? You need assurance that the grave is not the end, that there is life to come. You need hope for the future, something to take away the sting of death and the terror of the grave, something to dispel the darkness, the mystery of eternity. Jesus pleads with you: *I am the resurrection, and the life; he that believeth in me, though he were dead, yet shall he live; and whosoever liveth and believeth in me shall never die.* From the very first day that we discover ourselves, at some time during childhood, from the very first day we begin to feel our needs, to be burdened with our lives, to the last amen of a never ending eternity, the promises of God are a source of supply for all our needs, for everything we must have physically, mentally, morally, socially, economically, and especially spiritually. **Our lives are provided for in the promises of God. Our death is** anticipated in the promises of God. Eternity is provided for in the *exceeding great and precious promises* of God.

God's promises are *exceeding great and precious* not only because of their source, not only because of their scope, but because of their simplicity. Suppose a man needed a loan of ten thousand dollars. He would have to go to the bank, approach this secretary, interview that vice-president, sign this note and that mortgage. Suppose he had to have something from the President of the United States. We would probably never be able to see him. But the King of kings, the Lord of lords, is not like that. All you have to do is to think of Him — and there He is. When you want Him He is there. You do not have to sign a mortgage, and offer your life as collateral. Draw near unto Him. Step out on His promises. Claim them. See how simple they are. *Look unto me, and be ye saved, all ye ends of the earth: for I am God, and there is none else.* Look longingly, believingly to Jesus, and He will save you. *If ye abide in me, and my words abide in you, ye shall ask what ye will, and it shall be done unto you.* A child can understand this verse. *The wayfaring men, though fools, shall not err therein.* He that runs may read and believe and claim the Word. How mighty and how simple are these *exceeding great and precious promises! Seek ye first the kingdom of God, and his righteousness; and all these things shall be added unto you.* Whatever your problem, whatever your difficulty, whatever your need, bring it to God. You do not have to explain it. He understands. Ask Him for what you need. His love is more anxious to give than you are to receive.

You turn to me and say, "If these promises are so exceeding great and precious because of their source, because of their scope, because of their simplicity, why are Christians so poor, so feeble, so unhappy, so disturbed?" I will tell you a story. There was an Irish woman who had a son named Jack. He drank. One day while under the influence of drink he was shanghaied aboard a ship going to Australia. After the ship docked he went into the interior. He discovered a gold mine and became very rich. Jack loved his mother and wrote to her regularly, every two weeks. He told her how rich he was, about his wife, about his two children, his automobiles, his homes. The mother grew old and tired, but the son could not leave his business to see her. She finally became too feeble to work. The priest and the people of the parish decided that she must be sent to the poorhouse. The priest went to talk to her about it. They sat over their tea and small poor cakes, talking. The priest had befriended her for many years and knew she was a devout Catholic. This mission pained his heart. Finally he spoke.

"Daughter, I always wanted to ask you what became of your son. He left home. What happened to him? Do you ever hear from him?"

"Why, didn't I ever tell you?" she asked.

"No," he replied

"He went to Australia," the woman related. "He is very rich now. He has a wife and two children."

The priest asked, "How often do you hear from him?"

"Every two weeks, regularly."

"But doesn't he ever ask about your condition, what you are doing, how you are getting along, if you need any help?"

The woman shook her head. "No. He has never asked, and I never mentioned it. I did not want to worry him."

"Hasn't he ever sent you anything?"

"No, except for some small presents on my birthday and on the holidays."

"I can't understand it," said the priest. "He loves you. He has written you every two weeks during all these years. Yet he has never sent you a thing."

The woman replied, "No, except that in every letter there is a little greenish blue slip of paper."

The Catholic priest was no fool. "What did you do with these slips of paper?" he queried, surmising what they were.

"They looked so pretty. I have pasted them up in my bedroom."

They walked into the room. Pasted neatly from one side of the wall to the other, from the ceiling to the floor, were money orders covering thousands of dollars. That woman did not know what they were; so she plastered the wall with them. This woman was not nearly so foolish as those Christians who have the promises of God clearly stated in the Word and yet do not have enough faith to claim them. You may live on the mighty bounties of God. You may live on the fat things of Canaan. Your life may overflow with the abundance and superabundance of God's good things. Claim the promises of God. Endorse them by faith. God's bank is always open. It does not close its doors at three p.m., and on Sundays and holidays. Now, this minute, come to God. Acknowledge and accept Jesus Christ as your personal Saviour. Read the promises of God in the Bible. Claim your full part and portion in them by faith. God will do the rest. He is not straitened. He is not bankrupt. There is no inflation with Him. You will not embarrass Him by your frequent and great demands. Claim the fullness of God's bounties in the Name of the Lord Jesus Christ.

XIV
SAVED

And at midnight Paul and Silas prayed, and sang praises unto God: and the prisoners heard them. And suddenly there was a great earthquake, so that the foundations of the prison were shaken; and immediately all the doors were opened, and every one's bands were loosed. And the keeper of the prison awaking out of his sleep, and seeing the prison doors open, he drew out his sword, and would have killed himself, supposing that the prisoners had been fled. But Paul cried with a loud voice, saying, Do thyself no harm: for we are all here. Then he called for a light, and sprang in, and came trembling, and fell down before Paul and Silas, and brought them out, and said, Sirs, what must I do to be saved? And they said, Believe on the Lord Jesus Christ, and thou shalt be saved, and thy house. And they spake unto him the word of the Lord, and to all that were in his house. And he took them the same hour of the night, and washed their stripes; and was baptized, he and all his, straightway. And when he had brought them into his house, he set meat before them, and rejoiced, believing in God with all his house (Acts 16:25-34).

May this meditation help you to consider seriously the vital question *What must I do to be saved?* It is the most important question in all the Bible, in all the world. Problems beset us on every hand, but this is the most important of all. If you solve any other problem incorrectly you may suffer for it, but the consequences will not be eternal. However, this problem involves both time and eternity. Other decisions may be local, individual, but this query is universal.

This is a personal question. We cannot decide it for each other. We are not born in crowds. We do not die in crowds. We are not saved in crowds. We are not lost in crowds. One by one we must face Calvary, the death angel, the judgment, eternity.

This is a pressing question. There is no escaping it. There is no denying it. There is no hiding from it. There is no being indifferent to it. We must face it because it will

121

not let us escape from its implications. When it ceases to trouble us it is only because we have already accepted Jesus Christ as our Saviour, or have fallen so far into sin that the Spirit of God has stopped striving with us.

Because of the importance of this great thought, it behooves us to learn all we can of it, to study it thoroughly, to analyze it, to come to a definite decision regarding it. Let us, therefore, approach the question from three angles. First, why should we be saved? Second, what must we do to be saved? Third, when shall we be saved?

We should be saved, first, because of the value of our souls. In substance, each of us has a body, a mind, a soul. These three are all important, but the soul is by far the most important. There are many ways in which we can take care of our bodies. We can eat the right kind of food, take the proper exercise, sleep the required number of hours, spend time in the fresh air. Occasionally we need medicine. Sometimes a surgical operation is required. There are many ways in which we can provide for our bodies.

There are also many methods which we can employ in the training and care of the mind. We can go to school. We can study, read, meditate, listen to others, practice, exercise. It is perfectly proper, fully essential to see that our bodies and minds have the best of sustenance. But what about the soul? There is but one way to take care of the soul: by salvation. Nothing can touch the soul but the regenerating power of God's Holy Spirit.

One of these days our bodies will die. They will molder in some cemetery. Our minds will disintegrate with our bodies. But our souls will go on forever with God in heaven or the Devil in hell.

We should be saved, second, because of the difference between heaven and hell. Think of heaven's characteristics. It is a realm of life, of love, of light, of laughter. There is no sickness there, no sorrow, no suffering. There are no disappointments there, no disturbances, no discouragements. Wars are unknown. Want is vanquished. Woe is outlawed. The afflictions of the flesh do not prevail. It is the delightsome land of our fondest dreams, our loftiest imaginings.

Think of the company in heaven. God is there, and Christ, and the Holy Spirit. All the children who died in their infancy are there, rosebuds transplanted into the garden of God. The gentlest, the finest, the sweetest, the purest of the earth, those washed in the blood of the Lamb are there, forever serving God in His holy temple.

Think of what characterizes hell. It is a place of darkness, of torment, of eternal banishment from God, of pain, of anguish, of weeping, or unavailing remorse. Think of the company in hell. The vilest, the filthiest, the most corrupt, the most wicked in all creation are the denizens of the pit. People with whom you would shudder to associate compose hell's crowd. On earth you can choose your associates. In hell you are forever cast into the society of that awful bedlam, never to find release or relief from their lewdness, their corruption, their frightfulness. Yes, the difference between heaven and hell should lead you to seek salvation.

The third reason why we ought to be saved is this: the endlessness of eternity. If you could go to hell for a million years and then go to heaven, you would at last have deliverance. A million years would eventually pass. But heaven and hell are *forever*. The minute you accept Christ as your personal Saviour you start on the journey to heaven, never to finish until you stand complete, glorified in Christ before God, and establish your abode in the mansions of bliss forever and ever. If you reject Christ, there is nothing you can do in time or eternity that will keep or take you from the torment of hell or release you from it. *And the smoke of their torment ascendeth up for ever and ever:*

and they have no rest day nor night. That is a frightful
thought that should make all of us pause, that should constrain all of us to flee from the wrath to come. There is no
way out of heaven. There is no way out of hell.

The fourth reason why we ought to be saved is perhaps
not so self-centered and yet it is also eminently personal. It
is because of our influence upon others. There is not one of
you who would willingly, knowingly, consciously cause
anybody to stumble over your unbelief into destruction.
There is not one of you who would not gladly do anything,
everything to keep a soul out of hell and start it on the road
to heaven. You may if you wish. If you give your own heart
to the Lord Jesus Christ, surrender your own life to Him in
service, God will use you. God will bless and empower your
testimony. I do not care how weak, how small you think
yourself to be, God can and will use you to win others to
the Lord Jesus Christ. For these four reasons — the value
of your soul, the difference between heaven and hell, the
endlessness of eternity, your influence upon others — every
one of you ought to accept Jesus Christ as Saviour in this
very hour, then go out to live a consistent, consecrated,
fruit-bearing life, a truly Christian life.

What must we do to be saved? If I told you out of my
own heart or mind, if I gave you my own theological answer, you would have a right to hesitate, to question, to
doubt. But I will let God tell you what you must do. There
are three conditions essential for salvation. Regardless of
what anyone may say, the Bible is the Rule Book. There
are three things — not one, not two, but *three* — with which
you must comply ere you may consider yourself free from
all sin.

First, you must *repent. Seek ye the Lord while he may be
found, call ye upon him while he is near: let the wicked forsake his way, and the unrighteous man his thoughts: and*

let him return unto the Lord, and he will have mercy upon him; and to our God, for he will abundantly pardon (Isaiah 55:6-7). That is perhaps the Bible's clearest statement of this first requisite. You must turn your backs on your sins, on yourselves, on each other. You must turn your faces to God. In substance you must plead, "Lord, I know I am a sinner. I know I cannot save myself. I know Jesus Christ died for my sins. I know He can save me. Lord, have mercy on me a sinner."

The second step all of you know. The greatest statement of it is found in John 3:16: *For God so loved the world, that he gave his only begotten Son, that whosoever believeth in him should not perish, but have everlasting life.* You must believe in the Lord Jesus Christ. What does it mean to believe in Him? You must believe that He is the Son of God, that He died for your sins, that God raised Him from the dead, that He is sitting at the right hand of God, interceding for all of us, that He can save you, that He wants to save you, that He will save you if you trust Him.

There is one more thing you must do to be saved. You will find it mentioned in the Bible at least twice: once from the lips of Jesus and once from the pen of Paul. Jesus said, *Whosoever therefore shall confess me before men, him will I confess also before my Father which is in heaven.* Paul wrote, *That if thou shalt confess with thy mouth, the Lord Jesus, and shalt believe in thine heart that God hath raised him from the dead, thou shalt be saved. For with the heart man believeth unto righteousness; and with the mouth confession is made unto salvation* (Romans 10:9-10). You must confess Christ as your personal Saviour.

Our last question is: *When should we be saved?* Yesterday is gone. Some of you, perhaps, many of you, should have been saved yesterday, but yesterday is gone. It is too late to talk about it now. Not even God can call back those yesterdays. Shall you wait until tomorrow? How do you know you will be alive tomorrow? Will you want salvation more tomorrow than you do today? You know that every day of delay makes it just so much harder. Every day you postpone it you will want salvation less than the day before. How do you know God will want to save you tomorrow? Perhaps you say, "God will want to save me any time." That is not what my Bible says. It declares, *He, that being often reproved hardeneth his neck, shall suddenly be destroyed, and that without remedy . . . My spirit shall not always strive with man.* You dare not take a chance with God.

One night when I was conducting a revival, a boy came down the aisle, accepted Christ as his Saviour, and offered himself for baptism. The following Saturday night, a little before church time, he walked into his mother's room and spoke to her. "Mother, I have a terrible headache. I'm going to take my motorcycle and drive around awhile, and then go on to church." He used that motorcycle every day, and his mother saw no cause for concern. That night when I arrived home from church I received a call to "come quickly." Two motorcycle policemen cruising down the northwest highway had found the crushed motorcycle on one side of the road and the body of the boy on the other. He was dead. The following Tuesday his funeral was held. I attended. The church was crowded with people. Flowers were everywhere. There was barely room for the minister to stand in the pulpit. When the pastor told the story of the boy's stand for Christ, his friends thanked God for his conversion. His father and mother thanked God through their bitter tears that their son was saved. Supposing that boy had said, "Tomorrow." His soul would have gone down into hell — everlasting hell.

There is only one time to be saved and that is today.

There is only one time to repent and that is today. There is only one time to take a public stand for Christ and that is today. There is only one time today and that is *now*. There is only one time now and that is this hour. There is only one time this hour and that is this minute. Accept Christ as your personal Saviour *now*. Accept the offer of His matchless mercy *now*. Heed the call of the Spirit *now*. Say "yes" to God *now*. Step out on the Lord's invitation and promises *now*.

Dr. George Truett tells the following story again and again. He held a service in his own Junior Department in his own great church. He gave the invitation. Seventy Juniors came down the aisles for the Lord Jesus Christ. Most of them joined the church. Dr. Truett went about his business. That Thursday he received a telephone call from the Baylor Hospital in Dallas. A sick girl wanted to see him. The little girl, Nellie by name, was ill with influenza. Her father and mother were with her, and Doctor Truett led them in prayer. When he started for the door, the little girl — one of those who had accepted Christ on the previous Sunday — called him back.

"Will you do me a favor?" she asked.

"Certainly. What is it?"

"Will you go to my department Sunday and ask for me? If I am not there tell them where I am, and ask them to pray for me. Tell them Nellie said she wasn't afraid, because she has trusted Christ."

Sunday Dr. Truett saw that the child was not in Sunday school. He delivered her message and went on about his preaching. Saturday another telephone call came. Nellie was dying. Her parents wanted to see Dr. Truett. He rushed to the hospital, and found the mother and father standing at the foot of their little girl's bed, weeping. The child was stretched out on her back. Her eyes were closed, and her

face was pale with approaching death. Dr. Truett talked
quietly to her parents. After awhile the girl, opening her
eyes, saw her mother and father weeping. Moistening her
dry lips, in a hoarse, small voice, she asked, "Why are you
crying?"

They cried all the harder, naturally. Dr. Truett answered,
"Because you are going to leave them. You are going to
be with Jesus." It took her awhile to understand. In a
minute she understood.

"You mean I am going to die?" she asked.

"I'm sorry, but you are. You are leaving Daddy and
Mamma and going to heaven."

She closed her eyes and whimpered softly, too ill to cry
hard. Then she thought of something. Her face glowed
with smiles. Lifting herself on her elbows in her eagerness,
she said,

"I'm not afraid. I am a Christian. I am going to heaven.
Don't cry, Daddy. Don't cry, Mamma. The first thing I am
going to tell Jesus is how you both told me about Him, and
got me to love Him. I will be waiting for you. Don't cry.
Please don't cry."

She continued to comfort her mother and father. The
minutes ticked along. Her face grew more pale. She turned
to Dr. Truett. He got down on his knees and pressed his
ear against her lips. She was whispering.

"Will you go to my department again Sunday? I won't be
there, will I?"

"No. You will be in the Sunday school where Jesus is
Superintendent, and the angels are the teachers."

"Will you tell them where I am? Tell them I was not
afraid to die because I have trusted Christ. Tell them Nellie
said for all of them to give their hearts to Jesus, so when
they die they will not be afraid either."

That is Nellie's message to you. Oh, let it come into your

hearts. Let it fill your minds. Let it thrill your souls. Let it move your wills. You must be saved. God wants to save you. Jesus Christ died to save you. The Holy Spirit invites you to be saved. In this hour, this moment, right now, turn from your sins, put your faith in the Lord Jesus Christ, accept Him and confess Him as your personal Saviour. God for Christ's sake will do the rest. You will then be a child of God, and you will be saved eternally.

XV
GOD'S CHOSEN PEOPLE

But ye are a chosen generation, a royal priesthood, an holy nation, a peculiar people; that ye should shew forth the praises of him who hath called you out of darkness into his marvelous light: which in time past were not a people, but are now the people of God: which had not obtained mercy, but now have obtained mercy. Dearly beloved, I beseech you as strangers and pilgrims, abstain from fleshly lusts, which war against the soul; having your conversation honest among the Gentiles . . . Submit yourselves to every ordinance of man for the Lord's sake . . . For this is thankworthy, if a man for conscience toward God endure grief, suffering wrongfully . . . For even hereunto were ye called: because Christ also suffered for us, leaving us an example, that ye should follow his steps (I Peter 2:9-13, 19, 21).

Thank God there are myriads of Christians everywhere showing forth the praises of God, living in the will of God. a chosen generation, a royal priesthood, a holy nation, a peculiar people. The Holy Spirit who gives them the power so to live is available for every other Christian in the world. We may all be Christians whose lives prove an apt illustration of Peter's great appeal. The same holy, shining, burning, victorious testimony is available for each of us. The price is high but it is not beyond our ability to pay. Churches are composed of individual Christians. An effective church demands a consecrated membership. Each of us must be a professing, possessing, Christ-partaking, Christ-following child of God.

Without a single exception, throughout the ages of Christianity, the churches which have achieved this high position in God have had two things in common: a spiritual leadership and, at least in some measure, a spiritual membership. When I first started out to preach, not so very long ago, I had the idea that to have a great revival it was necessary for all the church members to be set on fire for Jesus. Experience has proved the fallacy of this belief. I say it out of a broken, aching heart. It seems utterly impossible in these last days for any church to be completely revived. Thank God, however, in almost every church there is a Master's minority which God can and does use for the advancement and upbuilding of His kingdom. The leaders of the church should always be from that minority.

The effectiveness of the church is determined by the devotion of those in official positions. It will be a terrible day when our backslidden, world-conforming, modernistic, prayerless, barren, fruitless leaders will have to give an accounting to the Lord Jesus Christ for the sheep of His pasture. If we have leaders whose lives are on the altar, just as surely as there is a God in heaven they will inspire other members who are willing to go the limit for Christ and the souls of men. Power attracts power. Zeal begets zeal. Compassion kindles compassion. True, in the very best of our churches there are only small Gideon bands. The history of Christianity has abundantly proved that a sacrificial leadership plus this Master's minority are more than sufficient to win the mightiest victories. The apostles were few in number. The Reformers were not many. The Wesleys and Whitefield could count their followers by the tens. Moody called out small prayer groups wherever he went. It seems that the Lord specializes in using the few to discomfit the many.

In these verses Peter gives us the secret of mighty Christian victory. They are eminently worthy of study, meditation and appropriation. The Holy Spirit indited these words in this burning testimony of the prince of the apostles. You will find three simple, definite thoughts for our consideration. These verses speak first of derivation; second, of designation; third, of destination.

Our derivation is: *Ye are a chosen generation.* The word "derivation" refers to our beginning, our origin. Clearly, our derivation is from God. Scripture specifically states this. Our Christian experience bears witness to this fact. It cannot come from below. It must come from above, through the exalted channel of the new birth.

Our derivation was purposed of God: *Blessed be the God and Father of our Lord Jesus Christ, who hath blessed us with all spiritual blessings in heavenly places in Christ: according as he hath chosen us in him before the foundation of the world, that we should be holy and without blame before him in love: having predestinated us unto the adoption of children by Jesus Christ to himself, according to the good pleasure of his will, to the praise of the glory of his grace, wherein he hath made us accepted in the beloved* (Ephesians 1:3-6).

God in His infinite wisdom and bountiful mercy purposed in Himself, before the foundations of the world were laid, that we were to be a chosen generation. God planned it before we were born, before time began, before the earth swung in space.

Our derivation was provided from above. We had nothing to do with the promise of redemption. We had nothing to do with the provision of salvation. We had nothing to do with the coming of the Lord Jesus Christ into the world to seek and to save that which was lost. We had nothing to do with the Passion of Calvary's Cross, with the emptying of Joseph's tomb, with the coming of the Holy Spirit. God provided this. Justification, adoption, sanctification were and are given us from above. Salvation is a gift, but it cost God the blood of His Son. Eternal life is the free gift of God's love, but it cost God the greatest treasure of time and eternity.

Just as utterly as we are dependent upon God for the

initiation of our salvation, just so completely are we dependent upon Him for the sustenance of our saved lives. Christ is the key to all the bounties of God. There is just one way to become a great Christian: to be in Christ. There is just one way to keep on being a great Christian: to continue in Christ. There is just one way to be effective in the service of the Lord: to be in Christ. There is just one way to win victory over sin, and Satan, and self: to be in Christ. There is just one way to be used of God in the greatest business of all the world, that of winning the souls of men: to be in Christ. Many of our people are insipid, indifferent, barren, fruitless because they have lost their connection with Christ. Power comes from God through the Holy Spirit. It is in Christ. The power of God that is able to do exceeding abundantly above all that we ask or think is available to us only in Christ.

Our designation beggars human language. *Ye are . . . a royal priesthood, an holy nation, a peculiar people.* There is no human position, no human pedestal, no human prestige that can elevate us to the honor and the glory contained in these words. We are a royal priesthood, called out, appointed, ordained, anointed, empowered by God to administer the mysteries of the Gospel and the sacrifices of God.

A *royal priesthood* implies, first of all, separation. The Levites were separated unto God. From their group Moses was directed to call out the family of Aaron for the priesthood. Just as Jesus was a Priest after the order of Melchizedek, even so are we priests after the order of Aaron. Our separation is in Christ, physically, mentally, morally, most of all spiritually. We are to be separated from the world, regardless of its attractions or affections. We are to be above all compromise. There must never be an unconfessed or unforgiven sin on our souls. In constant, unceasing penitence and confession we must seek and receive the cleansing blood of the Lord Jesus Christ.

A royal priesthood implies fellowship with God. We are invited by God to come into the holy of holies, to be in constant communion with Him. Were the President of the United States to choose one of us to be his continual companion, the honor would be great. But the Lord of lords, the King of kings, the God of the universe, Jehovah Himself, invites us to abide in His presence in sweet converse with Him. It is a wonderful thing to be a ruler of men, a great educator, a great scientist, a great physician, a great preacher, but the humblest Christian in unbroken fellowship with God has an infinitely more exalted position than all these combined.

A royal priesthood implies intercession before God. This is undoubtedly the greatest task, the loftiest duty, the mightiest privilege we Christians have. The lowliest Christian on his knees before God interceding for a lost world is doing a work that the angels covet. We do not properly emphasize intercessory prayer. It is our chief prerogative, our most definite responsibility, our most superlative opportunity, our most honorable work. A royal priesthood implies that by day and night we are to lift up the needs of a sin-driven world, the souls of a Devil-cursed universe, to the throne of God's compassionate grace. We serve God and our fellow men best on our bended knees.

Ye are . . . an holy nation — different from all the nations, kingdoms, principalities and ethnic groups of the world. God is our King. Christ is our Sovereign. The Holy Spirit is our Governor. We are ambassadors, not of the Court of Saint James, but of the Court of Eternal Glory. Our lives reflect credit or discredit, honor or dishonor on our heavenly citizenship. For example, if a group of Americans become drunk in Mexico, the Mexicans draw a distorted picture of all Americans. If a group of foolish Americans behave like swine in Paris, the French immediately conclude that all Americans are of that type. Someone has well said that the greatest argument for Christianity and the greatest argument against Christianity is a Christian life. If a minority of Christians in every church, in every denomination, would make concrete the teachings of our Lord and Saviour Jesus Christ, we would be in deed as well as in theory a holy nation; we would make such an impression upon our communities that revival fires would break out everywhere and people would cry out to us as they cried out to Peter and the other disciples, "Men and brethren, what must we do to be saved?"

We are a peculiar people. That word "peculiar" puzzled me for some time. I thought it designated an "odd" people. The original explains it. My tie clasp is peculiar to me. It belongs to me. My watch is peculiar to me. It belongs to me. We are a peculiar people, peculiar to God, because we belong to God. The more literal translation indicates "a peculiar possession," rather than "a peculiar people." We are God's possession. We are not our own. We have been purchased with a price beyond man's computation. All that we are, all that we have, our money, our talents, our time, our homes, our loved ones, our ambitions belong to God. Just as the Jews of old brought to God sacrifices of cattle and birds on the flaming, bleeding altars of the Temple, even so are we completely, totally, entirely to be burnt offerings at the feet of Jesus. That we are God's possession is a comforting thought. It means that we are under His care, in His will, sustained by His Word, provided for in His work. The world, the flesh and the Devil cannot overcome us. Satan had best leave us alone because of the punishment that God will wreak upon him for anything that he may do to us. We ourselves had better be exceedingly chary about what we do to each other, lest the wrath of God be kindled against us. If we are tempted to say aught against our pastors, our deacons, our fellow church members, it were best for us to speak in the secrecy of our closets on our knees before God. When we are tempted to criticize, to backbite, to gossip about our fellow Christians, we had better tell these things to the Lord when we kneel before Him, face to face, in the hour of devotion.

You will find our destination described in verses 11 through 21 of the passage which we are studying. Our destination refers to what God wants us to do, what we owe the Lord Jesus Christ, our church, our fellow men. First, we are to abstain from fleshly lusts. *Dearly beloved, I beseech you as strangers and pilgrims, abstain from fleshly lusts, which war against the soul.* "To abstain" means to stay away from, to fight shy of, to struggle against. Even the appearance of evil must be avoided. Resist the Devil and he will flee from you. We are to be spiritual athletes, buffeting our bodies, minds and souls, lest at any time we fall into the ways of the world and sin.

We are to have our conversation honest among the Gentiles. Our conduct with and before our fellow men must be crystal clear, unblotted, unstained, unblemished. Many preachers have hurt the cause of Christ by failing to pay their debts. Many deacons have cast evil aspersions upon the blessed Son of God by praying one way and living another. Many church members have gone to church on Sunday wearing an air of piety, then turned away to cheat and lie and steal during the weekdays. Some choir members sing like veritable angels in a cantata, then go out to carouse to the Devil's piping. Some Sunday school teachers stand before their classes Sunday morning and sit in a theater Sunday night. This will never do. This is not the way to have our conversation honest among the Gentiles.

We are to submit ourselves to every ordinance of man. Even small details are extremely important. We know that murder, thievery and adultery are wrong, but what about the laxity in the observance of other laws? A Christian is on constant parade. The Devil and the world are eager to mock him. Watch yourselves each day, each hour, each minute. You bear the brand of Christ. Remember that you are high-priced men. You have no business, even in the slightest way, to violate knowingly any law of man, regardless of what it may be. *Render to Caesar the things that are Caesar's and to God the things that are God's* is to be the guide for our lives. We must follow this rule carefully and exactly.

The ultimate expression of all this, the climactic result, the superimposed capstone is in these words: *For even hereunto were ye called: because Christ also suffered for us, leaving us an example, that ye should follow his steps.* Our derivation, our designation, our destination, the repression of ourselves, the expression of our religion, the impression of our love for God, of our passion for souls, the outcome of our service and activities — all are summed up in the command to be Christlike. Oh, to be Christlike! That should be the loftiest ambition, the constant hope, the abiding aspiration of every Christian. To magnify, to glorify, to gratify the Lord Jesus Christ must be the passionate yearning of every one of us who names the Name of Jesus as Christ and Lord. The Holy Spirit of God stands ready to spiritualize, energize, magnetize every one of us when and if we are willing to have Him use our lives, if we are willing to crown Jesus Lord of all.

One of these days we shall die. Our work will be over. Our possessions will be left behind. Our loved ones will be stopped at the gate that leads into the valley of the shadow of death. All of our efforts, all of our sacrifices, all of our trials, all of our achievements, all of our accomplishments, all of our possessions we shall leave behind. There will be one thing left that will go with us beyond the grave, that will stand for us at the judgment, that will reward us in an endless eternity, and that is the Christlikeness of our lives.

XVI
JESUS ONLY

And when they had lifted up their eyes, they saw no man, save Jesus only (Matt. 17:8).

Jesus only! That is the cry of eternity, the hope of the ages, the theme of the Bible, the bridge over hell, the gate into heaven. Jesus only is God's way, God's will, God's work for a lost world. The world has tried everything else. Would to God it would try Jesus. The world has tried education. Our penitentiaries, our divorce courts, our rogues' galleries are full of college graduates. Jesus only offers the knowledge of the truth which sets men free. The world has tried legislation. There are so many laws that the best of us at times advertently or inadvertently transgress them. These laws have merely added to the confusion of our age. They have been broken so often that they are mockeries. Jesus only with His law of grace can bind the human heart with the silken chains of gratitude and love to the chariot of God's will. The world has tried reformation. Projects, plans, programs, sanitation, segregation, schemes, undertakings ad infinitum, ad libitum, ad nauseam have crossed and recrossed each other. The world has spent billions of dollars, exerted mountain-moving energies, only to find that the soul of man is beyond the correction of any extraneous impressions. Jesus only is the Revealer of human sins, the Regenerator of human souls, the Ideal of human service. Jesus only is our message, our hope, our plea, our anchor.

Jesus is a Rock in a weary land,
A shelter in the time of storm.

Consider Jesus as the Saviour of your souls. You need this salvation. You must have that Saviour. Without Him all else is vain. With Him all things are part of a pattern of life that makes living worth-while, the past bearable, the present joyous, the future bright.

What have you without Christ? Your job? How long will you have it? What does it give you beside bread and butter, clothes, rent, money to pay your bills? If illness should come to you, of what help would your job be? If your loved one should become sick unto death, and the doctor should say, "Only God can help," of what value would your job be? When the death angel comes to require your soul, will your job help you? Will you pile your receipts and checks about your pillow and defy the angel of the Lord to make his way through them?

> For what is a man profited, if he shall gain the whole world, and lose his own soul? or what shall a man give in exchange for his soul?

What earthly possessions can compensate for the loss of eternal life? What mundane acquisitions can satisfy for the loss of the heavenly crown? What temporary advantages can pay for eternal banishment from the presence of God? What fleeting pleasures in this life can assuage the endless torments of a soul in hell?

What have you without Christ? Your loved ones? How long will you have them? Will you go first, or will they? Will the circle be unbroken? Will you meet beyond the open maw of the grave, beyond the chilling waters of stormy Jordan? Will the ties that bind you here on earth delay the germs of disease and of death? Will the strong arms of your passionate regard be strong enough to hold back the black-robed angel of death? Will your loved ones always be as gentle, as clean, as loyal, as pure, as affectionate as they are now? How many homes have been broken, hopes shattered, hearts crushed by the inroads of Satan into the edens that we have built for ourselves here upon the earth!

What have you without Christ? Your friends? They too will grow old and gray and weary. They too will be called to hear and to heed the last summons. Either you will precede them or they will precede you into the realms of eternity. Time and death will sever the dearest, the closest, the holiest ties on earth.

Jesus only is your eternal possession. Jesus only can give you immortality. Jesus only can forgive your sins. Jesus only can admit you into the bliss of divine fellowship. Jesus only can make you a child of the King. Jesus only can write your name in the Book of Life. Jesus only can cement your family circle with glory, salvation, safety. Jesus only can guarantee the reunion of friends in that bright home to come. Jesus only is the Saviour of your souls.

> Neither is there salvation in any other: for there is none other name under heaven given among men, whereby we must be saved.
> And she shall bring forth a son, and thou shalt call his name JESUS: for he shall save his people from their sins.

Consider Jesus only as your Source of stability. What hopes, what fears, what doubts, what questionings, what uncertainties possess us! In Christ we have a steadying influence. We know that His will is best for us. In the doing of it we find peace, rest, joy. We can come to His feet with our burdens. He will understand. Our prayers will find a ready response from His tender heart. Out of the turmoil and travail of our lives, out of the disturbances, the doubts, the discouragements, the disappointments that beset us on every hand, Jesus rises like the Rock of Gibraltar, the same yesterday, today, forever. He is the same in tenderness, in understanding, in sympathy, in loving, healing, life-giving, life-sustaining grace and power. The entire world is in a state of confusion. Dreams, hopes, institutions, eternal certainties which seemed to be basic, fundamental, foundational have crashed about us. The supposedly unshakable verities on which philosophers, economists, statesmen, diplomats, rulers, educators, even religious leaders have erected their scheme of things have been thwarted and twisted out of every semblance and shape of sanity. We are living in an Alice-in-Wonderland phantasmagoria. A fantastic nightmare has possessed the earth. Fear and trembling have assailed the souls of men.

Through it all, over it all, beyond it all, above it all is Jesus the Christ, the Son of God, the Lord of lords, the King of kings, the Prince of Peace, who is quietly, slowly, certainly, eternally working out the destinies of men, of nations, of an entire universe, to conform to His holy, perfect will. Anchor your souls in the haven of rest. When you build your life on the Rock of Ages and center your activities in the will, the work, the way, aye, the Word of Christ Jesus, the world stops whirling about; fears vanish; doubts disappear; discouragements evaporate; disappointments become His appointments; life takes on new meaning. We know from whence we have come, whither we are going, what we shall find when we get there. Even the needs of the way are amply supplied. The puzzle of life is solved when we come to know at the feet of Jesus that *all things work together for good to them that love God, to them who are the called according to his purpose,* and when we abide by this command: *Seek ye first the kingdom of God, and his righteousness; and all these things shall be added unto you . . . Whatsoever ye do, do all to the glory of God.*

In my seminary days, the matchless Dr. Claggett Skinner of Virginia addressed us in chapel one day. He told a story. One Monday, after an unusually trying Lord's Day, this great preacher saddled his horse and turned his back on the town for a quiet, God-communing ride in the woods. He chose a path at random, dropped the reins on the horse's neck and rode on. Minute after minute the animal picked its way through the thickets. The preacher was lost in a brown study. Suddenly the horse stopped. The preacher looked up. The horse had brought him into a cleared space. At one end of it was an old, weather-beaten, tumbledown shack with a small cleared garden space beside it. In front of the house on a rickety, backless chair sat an aged negro woman smoking a corncob pipe. The preacher got off the horse, dropped the reins over its head and walked over toward the woman. She did not look up until the shadow of his body fell on her. She lifted her head, squinted her rheumy old eyes, looked down again and continued to smoke her pipe. Dr. Skinner bent over her.

"Mammy, are you here all alone?" he asked.

She made no reply but smoked placidly. Again the preacher bowed to look into her lined face.

"Mammy," he said, speaking more loudly, "are you here alone?"

Once more the old negress lifted her head. This time she took the corncob pipe from her mouth. Deliberately she moistened her lips. "Jes' me and Jesus," she said softly. Then, after a moment she repeated, "Jes' me and Jesus, massa. Jes' me and Jesus."

Dr. Skinner said that the empty glade became peopled with the hosts of heaven as the almost whispered syllables of that black child of God fell on his ears. God was there, and Christ, and the Holy Spirit. The angels were there, messengers of God and grace, attending to the wants of that aged saint. That is right. "Just me and Jesus" abundantly satisfies. "Just me and Jesus" against the world! "Just me and Jesus" against sorrow, suffering, sickness! "Just me and Jesus" against sin and Satan! "Just me and Jesus" against death and the grave! "Just me and Jesus" for all eternity, here and hereafter! "Just me and Jesus!"

Finally, consider Jesus as the Surety for your supplies. We all have a life to live, a death to die, an eternity to enjoy. Jesus is the Surety behind the promises of God. In Him they are all yea and amen. He is the channel through which flow the abundant blessings and bounties of God. He is the rich store of all the manifold benedictions which God has for those who come to Him through Christ.

Jesus is the Surety for our pardon, for our forgiveness. The Book is explicit on that point. *Be it known unto you therefore, men and brethren,* cries Paul, *that through this man is preached unto you the forgiveness of sins: and by him all that believe are justified from all things, from which ye could not be justified by the law of Moses . . . In whom we have redemption through his blood, the forgiveness of sins, according to the riches of his grace . . . Wherefore he is able also to save them to the uttermost that come unto God by him, seeing he ever liveth to make intercession for them.* Can words be more definite, more simple, more direct? Can promises be more universal, more unconditional? Can offers be more inclusive, more inviting, more inspiring? Surely this Jesus only is the Surety for the forgiveness of our sins, for the blotting out of our transgressions, for the taking away of our iniquities. Surely with such bountifully blessed syllables falling from the very heart of God, none need fear a welcome, a relief, a release through the efforts, energies and achievements of the Lord Jesus Christ.

Jesus only is the Surety for our peace, for our fellowship with God. *But as many as received him,* says John, inspired by the Holy Spirit, *to them gave he power to become the sons of God, even to them that believe on his name.* Paul continues the story: *For as many as are led by the Spirit of God, they are the sons of God. For ye have not received the spirit of bondage again to fear; but ye have received the spirit of adoption, whereby we cry, Abba, Father . . . Jesus answered and said unto him, If a man love me, he will keep my words: and my Father will love him, and we will come unto him, and make our abode with him.* It is only in the Lord Jesus Christ that we can enjoy constant communion with God. It is only in the Lord Jesus Christ that the Spirit bears witness with our spirits that we are children of God. It is only in the Lord Jesus Christ that God speaks to us words of comfort, of counsel, of conquest. Jesus only, as He clasps us to the heart of God, is our bulwark, strong, unassailable, unchangeable, against the onslaughts, the trials, the tribulations that are the common lot of every one of us. The difficulties of life, the pressure of circumstances, the burdens of the world drive us to the feet of Him who understands, who knows, who loves. It is there that we find peace and rest for our souls. The sunshine of His smile, the sweetness of His words, the safeness of His prevailing presence greet us with unwearying, unfailing tenderness.

Jesus only is the Surety for our power. This is the meaning of Paul's *Christ hath redeemed us from the curse of the law, being made a curse for us: for it is written, Cursed is every one that hangeth on a tree: that the blessing of Abraham might come on the Gentiles through Jesus Christ; that we might receive the promise of the Spirit through faith.* This promise is universal, effective, available. It is only in Jesus that we have its fruition and accomplishment. Jesus only bestows upon us not only the pardon of our sins but the fullness of the power of the regenerating spirit, so that we may be more than conquerors through Him that loved us. It is the Spirit, the free gift of God's love through Christ, who bestows upon us all the blessings that flow from God's grace. Wisdom, courage, inspiration, enthusiasm, Scriptural understanding, power to pray, to preach, to bear witness, to build up the kingdom, to win souls — all are contained in the abundance of the Holy Spirit. He cannot be bought. He cannot be constrained. He cannot be earned. Like salvation, He must be received as the free gift of God's grace.

Jesus only is the Surety for our promotion, for our coronation. Jesus only is the password to the mansions of glory, the title deed to the home in the skies. Jesus himself said, *I am the resurrection, and the life; he that believeth in me, though he were dead, yet shall he live: and whosoever liveth and believeth in me shall never die . . . Let not your heart be troubled: ye believe in God, believe also in me. In my Father's house are many mansions: if it were not so, I would have told you. I go to prepare a place for you. And if I go and prepare a place for you, I will come again, and receive you unto myself; that where I am, there ye may be also. And whither I go ye know, and the way ye know. Thomas saith unto him, Lord, we know not whither thou goest; and how can we know the way? Jesus saith unto him, I am the way, the truth, and the life: no man cometh unto the Father, but by me.* Eternity speaks in these words. Heaven itself grows still as their sound rings out to the souls of men. These words are definite, unchangeable, eternal. When God has accomplished His purpose in us here upon this earth, when we have done our last bit of work for Christ, there is waiting for us a heavenly reward that is reserved for all those who love Christ and wait for His appearing. No wonder that vacillating, oscillating, hesitating, denying Peter, having recognized Jesus only, could cry to the ages, *Blessed be the God and Father of our Lord Jesus Christ, which according to his abundant mercy hath begotten us again unto a lively hope by the resurrection of Jesus Christ from the dead, to an inheritance incorruptible, and undefiled, and that fadeth not away, reserved in heaven for you, who are kept by the power of God through faith unto salvation ready to be revealed in the last time.* The same driving force that stabilized and assured Peter's faith is ours for the taking through Jesus only.

For nineteen hundred years this Gospel of Jesus only has been preached to the children of men of all climes, continents, conditions, circumstances. Multiplied multitudes have found in Jesus only the Saviour of their souls, the Stabilizer of their lives, the Surety of their supplies. God offers Him to you this hour. Will you have Him? The decision is yours. Your past, your present, your future, your body, your mind, your soul, your spirit, your life, your death, your eternity depend on what you do with this Jesus only. He brings you the gold of Ophir, the wealth of the Indies. He offers you the blood of cleansing, the water of salvation, the bread of life. Today, by yielding yourself to Jesus only, by accepting His offer, by surrendering to His will, you may become a child of the King, a prince of the blood, an heir of eternity. With outstretched hands and pleading voice Jesus invites and urges you to come to Him now. Will you say with the poet—

> I'll go to Jesus tho' my sin
> Like mountains round me close;
> I know His courts I'll enter in
> Whatever may oppose.
>
> Prostrate I'll lie before His throne
> And there my guilt confess;
> I'll tell Him I'm a wretch undone
> Without His sov'reign grace.
>
> I can but perish if I go;
> I am resolved to try;
> For if I stay away I know
> I must forever die.

But you will not perish. Jesus only stands ready, willing, eager, anxious, yearning, gracious, abundantly able to save you, to cleanse you, to free you, to use you, to take you to

Himself forever in glory when He has accomplished His purpose in you here upon earth. Come to Jesus. Come to Jesus *now*.

XVII
THE SAVIOUR'S INVITATION

Come unto me, all ye that labour and are heavy laden, and I will give
you rest (Matthew 11:28).
Him that cometh unto me I will in no wise cast out (John 6:37b).

In one of D. L. Moody's sermons there is a moving story.
A man, steeped in sin and convicted of the evil of his soul,
came to the great evangelist seeking the way of salvation.
Moody opened his Bible to John 6:37 and pointed to these
words: *Him that cometh unto me I will in no wise cast out.*
The man raised the objection: "Brother Moody, I am a
drunkard." "It does not say," replied Moody, " 'Him that
cometh unto Me who is not a drunkard I will in nowise cast
out.' " The man said, "Brother Moody, I have abandoned
my wife and my children," "That is a dreadful sin, man,"
replied Moody, "but it does not say, 'Him that cometh unto
Me who has not abandoned wife and children I will in nowise cast out.' " The man presented a third objection:
"Brother Moody, I have stolen; I have been in jail." "Still,
brother," softly countered Moody, "it does not say, 'Him
that cometh unto me who has never stolen, who has never
been in jail, I will in nowise cast out.' It merely says, *Him
that cometh unto me I will in no wise cast out.* That covers
you without argument or exception." The man was convicted, believed, gave his poor sinful heart to Christ and
went on his way rejoicing.

Beloved, Christ stands ready to receive you just as you
are. You need not hesitate. You need not delay. You need
not wait for more faith, for more feeling. Come with your
doubts. Come with your questions. Come with your little

faith. If you have enough faith to make you realize your need of Christ and His ability to help you, that is all He asks.

> Let not conscience make you linger
> Nor of fitness fondly dream.
> All the fitness He requireth
> Is to feel your need of Him.

There are no reservations in it. There are no conditions to be met. It means just what it says: *Come unto me, all ye that labour and are heavy laden, and I will give you rest . . . Him that cometh to me I will in no wise cast out.* It is beyond doubt, beyond comparison, beyond question the greatest invitation in the entire Bible, the Saviour's supreme invitation. It is all-inclusive in its blanket broadness. Every man, woman and child in all the world is included in it. It is so simple that the wayfarer, though a fool, may not err therein, so clear that a child can easily understand its meaning. There is nothing for us to do except to believe, to receive, to claim. Its terms are so definite that there is no room for doubt or difficulty.

The invitation is not only simple, not only inclusive, not only definite, not only positive, but it is pressingly present. Just as John the Baptist came when he cried, *Behold the Lamb of God, which taketh away the sin of the world;* just as Peter came when he said, *Thou art the Christ, the son of the living God;* just as Bartimaeus came when he prayed, *Thou Son of David have mercy on me;* just as the Ethiopian eunuch came when he confessed, *I believe that Jesus Christ is the Son of God,* even so you may come and welcome.

There are three tremendous thoughts in this mighty text. They are very clear and appropriate. First, the text speaks of man's part, the need: . . . *all ye that labour and are heavy laden.* Second, it tells us of God's part, the invitation: *Come unto me.* Third, it speaks of Christ's part, the promise: *I will give you rest . . . Him that cometh unto*

me I will in no wise cast out. You and I are the invited.
God issues the invitation. Christ fulfills the promise.

Man's part is the load, the sin, the corruption, the need.
We all labor and are heavy-laden. We all have our burdens.
Some of us have many burdens, some of us have few, but
there are none of us without them, without difficulties, without trials, without heartaches. I am a Jew. I used to be a
lawyer. I have known rich Jews, poor Jews, educated Jews,
ignorant Jews. I have known rich Gentiles, poor Gentiles,
educated Gentiles, ignorant Gentiles. I have met all sorts
of people under all sorts of circumstances and conditions.
I have come to the very definite conclusion that all men
alike, Jews and Gentiles, are hungrily, anxiously, search-
ing for two things. They are looking for security. They
are looking for peace. We all want to know that we will
have enough to eat, that we will have a roof over our heads,
clothing on our backs, a bed in which to sleep. We want to
be sure that we will have enough money to pay our debts,
to clothe, feed, educate and provide a home for our children.
We want to know that our health will permit us to work and
earn our daily bread. We want security. We are troubled
without it.

We also want peace — peace with God, peace with ourselves, peace with each other. This is the primal need of
every human soul. Nothing can take its place. You will
find this hunger for peace in the most unlikely places, in
the most unlikely people. I have known men powerful in
the affairs of the world whose lives were filled with the fury
of turmoil. I have known women with the world at their
feet troubled and tormented in their souls. Peace is the cry
of the human heart.

Where shall we find security? Will money obtain it? Will
a good job, a comfortable or even luxurious home, social
position, political preferment, economic prestige obtain

them for us? We all know better than that. During recent years those things we have held most stable have crashed at our feet. Institutions, organizations, practices, programs seemingly built on secure foundations have been smashed by the onslaught of world-twisting forces. Money has failed. Education has been found to be but a will-o'-the-wisp. Great leaders of every nation under the sun — honest, sincere, anxious, hardworking leaders — have stood helplessly by to see their countries bleeding, torn, wasted, unhappy, uncertain, depressed, distressed, degraded, diseased, discouraged, destroyed. Surely these times have proved that there is nothing secure in this world.

Where shall we find peace? Will property insure it? Will pleasures provide it? Did Lindbergh's millions help him when his son was kidnaped and slain? Did President Calvin Coolidge's powerful position help him when his boy died in Walter Reed Hospital? What peace, and for what duration, can this world and all the things in it give to us? When sickness comes, when sorrow attacks, when suffering is the rule of the day, when loved ones pass on to the great beyond, when our own time comes to face the Grim Reaper, what then? Shall we gather about us our pleasures, our money, our degrees, our stocks, our bonds, our honors, our emoluments and find peace in them? Beloved, it cannot be done. It has been tried many times. God give me the grace to tell you this, and may He grant you the grace to receive it. When your time comes to die, when my time comes to die, we will begrudge every minute, every penny, every effort we spent in any other way except in the service and in the fellowship of Christ.

Dr. Truett relates this incident in one of his great sermons. A wealthy young cotton broker was an active member of his church. The man had a wife and a little girl. I do not know why God did it, but when the child was about seven years of age she died of diphtheria. Because of sanitary laws, her funeral was held in the cemetery, and numerous friends and relatives gathered about the little grave. Dr. Truett preached one of his inimitable sermons, opening the very gates of heaven to show Christ's warm reception and welcome of that precious soul. When the benediction was pronounced, the undertaker prepared to lower the coffin into the grave. The father stopped him. Kneeling down, he pressed a little silver key into the lock of the coffin and opened it. Some minutes he knelt looking down into the still white face of his child. Bending, he gently pressed his lips to the cold baby lips. Closing the coffin, locking it, putting the little silver key back into his pocket, he rose to his feet and, linking his arm in Dr. Truett's arm, walked to the car where the grief-stricken mother was waiting. As the two came along, the man leaned heavily on Dr. Truett's arm and, in a voice heavy, weary, grief-stricken, said, "Brother Truett, she was all I had." This statement was not entirely true. He had his wife. He had his business. He had his home. But, beloved, his peace was buried with that darling of his heart. All else was of no avail.

That may not be your problem. Our needs vary. Peace and security may come to us in different ways. Our trials are of various sorts. Some of us are tired physically. Some of us are burdened mentally. Some of us have financial difficulties. No matter what we may face, what afflictions may affect us, the greatest problem of every one of us, the greatest labor, the greatest burden, is spiritual. We need God. We need Christ. We need the forgiveness of our sins. We need the regeneration of our souls. We need the Holy Spirit. We need our names written in the Book of Life. We need the assurance of immortality, of the resurrection from the dead, of the hope of a home in heaven. You recall that when the disciples came back after their first evangelistic tour of Palestine to report to Christ they said, *Lord, even the devils are subject unto us through thy name.* The Lord answered and said unto them, *Notwithstanding in this rejoice not, that the demons are subject unto you; but rather rejoice, because your names are written in heaven.*

The second part of the text speaks of an invitation: *Come unto me* is God's invitation. It is not the Church, not the Christian, not the Bible, not a preacher that extends this invitation to you. God gives you this invitation. I am merely a messenger, a representative, an ambassador. My poor voice is echoing the mighty voice of God, calling unto you. My only concern, my deep concern, my passionate concern is that I may give you God's invitation. Think with me of the many ways in which God appeals to your hearts. Look into the sky. The sun, the moon, the twinkling, glittering stars, the fleecy clouds—all are the messengers of God. Nature in every one of its mighty wonders, in all of its magnificent beauty, is the hand of God beckoning to your soul. There is not a work of God in time or in space that has not as its definite primary purpose to bring you to the great beating Overheart.

God has also written His invitation on the tablets of your conscience. By day and by night, at home and abroad, in sin and out of sin, in the most unlikely places, the most unlikely circumstances, under the inspiration of some song or sermon, some word, some providential occurrence, the still small voice within us pleads the Lord's cause. Not until we have committed the unpardonable sin, not until by indifference and unbelief or even by overt rejection we have driven the Holy Spirit from us does that voice stop striving, does that voice loose its patient power. Conscience is the word of eternity implanted in our souls to remind us that we are bound for death and judgment, and must make our peace, our calling, our election sure.

God has written His invitation on almost every page of the Bible. There is no story, there is no promise, there is no doctrine, there is no type, there is no proclamation that does not contain somewhere within it God's hand and heart reaching out for us. Some one has found that the word "Come" is mentioned 642 times in the Book. Just think of it, beloved! So anxious is God about our welfare that 642 times He asks us to come, invites us to share in His bounty.

This invitation is pressed upon us through the prayers, the tears and the testimonies of our loved ones, of our friends, of our Christian neighbors. Thank God, they will not leave us alone. They keep after us. We refuse them. We abuse them. We break their hearts and crush their souls, but these dear children of God keep on praying, keep on begging, keep on wooing. Thank God a thousand times for those who persistently sought us out and as persistently pressed the claims of the Redeemer upon us.

But clearer than the voice of nature, more definite than the word of conscience, superior even to the testimonies of the Bible, exceeding in force the prayers, the tears, the efforts of preachers and Christian friends is the blood-red invitation God wrote in the shame, the loneliness, the heartache, the heartbreak, the death of Jesus Christ. On the Cross of Calvary the Almighty exhausted all His plans, all His purposes, all His programs, all His powers to assure us of His love, to invite us to His grace, to welcome us to His mercy. Christ is a portrait of the longing heart of God. It is by His bloodstained Cross that I invite you to come to God.

A young girl living in a Western town quarreled with her mother. She left home in a rage and went to New York City. Tired of working, or perhaps unable to find work, she descended into deep sin. She drank. She caroused. Her life was steeped in iniquity. The mother continued to weep and pray over her prodigal daughter. She tried every means to locate the young woman and bring her home. Finally, at the suggestion of her pastor, she had a number of photographs made of herself and scattered them from one end of the country to the other. She sent them to hotels, to mission halls, to Y.W.C.A.'s, with the hope and prayer that the girl would see one of them and be moved to return. Across the front of every picture she wrote two words: "Come home." She signed the message "Mother."

One night the girl returned home half drunk from a wild orgy. As she staggered along she passed the lighted window of a mission. Glancing at it, she saw a photograph across the page of an open Bible. The girl walked past but something pulled her back. The face on the picture was strangely familiar. It was late and the mission was locked. The next day she came back and the mission director told her that it was her mother. He had recognized the girl from the description on the back of the photograph. The pathetic expression on the mother's face broke the heart of the daughter, and in the mission she wept out her repentance and remorse. The superintendent somehow raised enough money to pay the girl's fare to her home. Buying her ticket, he put her on the homeward-bound train. Arriving at her destination, the girl stepped off the train and walked down the street to her home. Her heart was heavy. Her soul was torn. She did not know what to expect. Hesitantly she knocked on the door. The mother threw open the door, recognized the daughter, and with passionate tears and kisses gave the girl her love and forgiveness. There was no criticism, no abuse. The aching, longing, yearning heart of the mother was filled with grace and compassion for the daughter, and the pain and bitterness of the terrible months spent in sin were forgotten.

Beloved, this story portrays the love of God. He wants

us home. If you accept His invitation, He will not talk about your sins, but about your salvation. He will not discover your shortcomings, but speak of your sanctification. There will be no abuse; there will be no remonstrance. The patient heart of God will press you to itself. He will kiss away the stains of your soul. He will strip you of the rags of evil and clothe you in the robes of righteousness. He will put the ring of adoption upon your finger and the shoes of satisfaction on your feet. He will call the angels together to rejoice over a sinner who has come home.

There is a third part to this text, the promise of Christ: *I will give you rest . . . Him that cometh unto me I will in no wise cast out.* This is the sweetest portion of the entire story. The ages have proved that it is true. It is inspiration to the longing soul, comfort to the burdened heart, calm to the troubled mind. Let us rejoice as we think upon this glorious promise.

Remember Christ's accessibility. He is always ready to receive you. When you go to visit some public official you must first see his secretary. You cannot visit the governor of the state unless you have an introduction. If need were to drive you to the President of the United States you would have to answer many questions and contact many people before you could have an audience with him. It is not so with Christ. He is always accessible. You can go to Him at any time and know that He is eager to receive you. The record of the New Testament proves that by day and by night, to the young, to the old, to the good, to the bad, to the rabbi, to the rabble, Jesus was ever available. There is no need of an intermediary. There is no need of a recommendation or an introduction. Just as you are, Jesus is waiting to help you, to welcome you.

Consider also Christ's longing for your response. Some years ago a young couple lost their seven-year-old daughter.

The wife was disconsolate, brooding, and grieving over the death of her baby. The doctor and the young husband decided it might help the mother if the couple adopted a little child. It took the husband some time to persuade her to take that step. Finally she consented, but with the understanding that the child would have to resemble their departed darling. They went to an orphanage and discussed the matter with the superintendent, and showed him the picture of their deceased child. The superintendent brought out ten or twelve little girls between the ages of six and eight, each of them blond, curly-haired, blue-eyed, each of them resembling somewhat the departed one.

The mother selected a little girl and asked the husband and the superintendent to lead the others away. She wanted to be alone with the child which she had chosen. When the others had gone she picked up the little orphan and placed her on the piano bench. Gently, tenderly she talked to the somewhat frightened child, told her about her own dear loved one, and asked her if she would like to come home with her and be her little girl.

"If you come to our house, darling," she said, "we are rich, and you can have everything you want. You will have a nursery, a governess, a pony, many dolls, pretty dresses, toys, as many as you can use."

The girl stood with her little head bowed, her hands hanging down at her sides. She said not a word. The woman continued to plead, promise, love, beg. The little girl remained mute. The mother talked about a trip to Europe, which the family was planning, about all the playmates she would have, about all the good times that would be hers. The child remained silent. Finally the mother dropped her arms to her sides and stepped back, defeated.

Then the little girl raised her head, her eyes were filled with unshed tears as she asked, "If I come and be your little girl, and you give me all these things, what do you want me to do, lady?" The mother sprang forward. Pressing her arms around the little girl, she hugged her close to her heart, and sobbed as she said, "Darling, all we want you to do is just to love us, just to love us."

Beloved, I have searched the Bible through and through. I have prayed over it. I have wept over it. I have rejoiced over it. I have tried to find in its pages God's will for my life. Neither in the Old Testament nor in the New have I located anything that God asks me to do more than just to love Him. Brethren, every line of its thousands of pages is an echo of the great beating heart of Christ saying, *Lovest thou me?* How can anyone refuse such a cry? How can anyone reject such a Christ? Think of all that He has done for us. Think of the price that He paid for our salvation. Think of the little that He asks in return. Today respond to His yearning love by accepting Him as your personal Saviour. That is what He wants. That is what He asks. That is what He seeks. He does not want your money. He does not want your possessions. He does not want your toil. He wants your heart. He wants *you.* He does not want to take aught from you. He wants you to give all, of your own loving will. Respond to his love. Tell Him that you love Him. Look up into His face and say, "Thank You, Lord Jesus, for Calvary, for the Cross, for the nails, for the blood. Thank You for the thousands of other blessings you have bestowed on me."

Some years ago there lived an old widowed mother, past eighty, in a small town in Iowa. She had several great-grandchildren. Her oldest son was sixty-seven years of age, and a grandfather. Her children, grandchildren and great-grandchildren decided to surprise her with a reunion to be held on Christmas Day. From all over the state they came that day. They hid in the warm barn until all had arrived.

At last in a group they rushed into her room, shouting, "Surprise! Surprise!" The aged saint's heart was full of joy. What talk, what laughter, what rejoicing, what singing they had that holiday!

The hours sped along, and evening shadows began to creep. The children started to scatter to their homes. One by one they came into the grandmother's room to kiss her good-bye. The last one to come was her oldest son. As he walked into the room and stepped over the threshold, he noticed her sitting looking out of the window, her hands quietly folded in her lap. She did not hear him. He stood there watching her. Those old wrinkled hands that had worked so hard, that had taken such tender care of him, that dear wrinkled face that had bent over him so many sleepless nights, broke his heart. He tiptoed over to his mother, and knelt beside her. Putting his head in her lap as he had done long ago when he was a small boy, he remained there for several minutes. Running her fingers through his sparse gray hair, the mother patted him tenderly, gently. After a time he raised his head and, looking into the dear mother's dimmed eyes, said, "Mother, I sure do love you!" The old lady pressed her boy's face between her two hands, kissed him on the lips, and said, "Son, I have been waiting sixty-seven years for you to tell me that."

This desire is also in the soul of God. It is the longing of any earthly father, of any earthly mother. I have two tiny children, a boy and a girl. I want them to have all that I can give them. They can have my strength, my blood, my time, my thought, my money. All I want in return from both of them is some day to hear them say, "Daddy, I sure do love you!" That is pay enough. I want nothing else.

I believe that this yearning for response is in the heart of Christ. He is anxious about you. He wants to give you the choicest, the best of all that He has. He wants you to draw unstintingly on His bounty. He wants to forgive your sins, to fill you with the Spirit, to answer your prayers, to keep you, to comfort you, to sustain you, to supply your needs in this life, to take you to Himself in heaven when your work on earth is finished.

He will give you an unqualified and assured welcome. He wants you to come just as you are, without waiting for anything or anybody. He has all that you need in superabundance. He can do exceedingly, abundantly above all that you ask or think in every problem of your life. You need not hesitate. He knows your need. He knows your condition. His invitation is directed to you. His promise is yours for the taking. He has never broken any promise He has spoken, and He will not break this promise to you. This moment say and act upon the words of that matchless invitation hymn:

> Just as I am, without one plea,
> But that Thy blood was shed for me,
> And that Thou bidd'st me come to Thee,
> O Lamb of God, I come! I come!

XVIII

PLAIN GOSPEL FOR PLAIN PEOPLE

But what saith it? The word is nigh thee, even in thy mouth, and in thy heart: that is, the word of faith, which we preach; that if thou shalt confess with thy mouth the Lord Jesus, and shalt believe in thine heart that God hath raised him from the dead, thou shalt be saved. For with the heart man believeth unto righteousness; and with the mouth confession is made unto salvation. For the Scripture saith, Whosoever believeth on him shall not be ashamed. For there is no difference between the Jew and the Greek: for the same Lord over all is rich unto all that call upon him. For whosoever shall call upon the name of the Lord shall be saved (Romans 10:8-13).

The salvation discussed in these simple verses of Scripture is needed by all. It is intended for all. It is within the reach of all. It may be secured by all. There are various offers of salvation in the Bible. Isaiah 45:22 declares: *Look unto me, and be ye saved, all the ends of the earth: for I am God, and there is none else.* The fullness of salvation is ours for a look. Isaiah 55:6, 7 tells us: *Seek ye the LORD while he may be found, call ye upon him while he is near: let the wicked forsake his way, and the unrighteous man his thoughts: and let him return unto the LORD, and he will have mercy upon him; and to our God, for he will abundantly pardon.* In Matthew 11:28 we read: *Come unto me, all ye that labour and are heavy laden, and I will give you rest.* John 1:12 tells us: *But as many as received him, to them gave he power to become the sons of God, even to them that believe on his name.* John 3:14-16 says this: *And as Moses lifted up the serpent in the wilderness, even so must the Son of man be lifted up: that whosoever believeth in him should not perish, but have eternal life. For God so loved the world, that he gave his only begotten Son, that whosoever believeth in him should not perish, but have everlasting life.* John 5:24 states: *Verily, verily, I say unto you, He that heareth my word, and believeth on him that sent me, hath everlasting life, and shall not come into condemnation; but is passed from death unto life.* In Acts 16:31 we read: *And they said, Believe on the Lord Jesus Christ, and thou shalt be saved, and thy house.* Revelation 3:20 contains this glorious promise: *Behold, I stand at the door, and knock: if any man hear my voice, and open the door, I will come in to him, and will sup with him, and he with me.*

In the thirteenth verse of the tenth chapter of Romans, *For whosoever shall call upon the name of the Lord shall be saved,* which is part of my text, is the simplest, the clearest, the easiest to understand of them all. There are three great thoughts in it: first, the universal offer of salvation; second, the universal condition of salvation; third, the universal promise of salvation.

The universal offer of salvation is contained in the word "whosoever." There are no national restrictions. The Jew, the Gentile, the American, the European, the Asiatic, the African, the man from the islands of the sea — all need Christ; all are included in the Gospel; all are offered salvation by Christ. Some years ago I found myself in the First Baptist Church in Lawton, Oklahoma, in a Baptist associational workers' meeting. It was a drowsy afternoon. The proceedings were rather dull. Report after report had been read to the sleepy assemblage. Suddenly the moderator called out, "Appelman, come up here." I came to the front of the church and stood at the pulpit to shake hands with the presiding officer.

"Girgis, you come here." From the right side of the auditorium there stepped out towards the pulpit a slender, dark-faced, narrow-eyed, kinky-haired Egyptian.

"Appelman, do you know Girgis? Girgis, do you know Appelman?"

"Yes," replied the two. We know each other. We have been prayer partners in the seminary."

"Hays!" called the moderator, "you come here also." From the middle of the auditorium there arose a strong-looking, clean-faced, barely middle-aged preacher, and he also took his place before the group.

Hays, Girgis and Appelman shook hands. One was a Russian-born Jew. The second was an Egyptian-born Copt. The third was an Irish American. They were all Christians, Baptists, preachers of the Gospel. Beloved, I submit to you that only in Christ, only in the Gospel, only in salvation could these three have met on equal terms.

There are no material restrictions. The rich man, the poor man, the beggar, the thief — all have sinned and come short of the glory of God. They all need the blood of Calvary's Cross to make them fit and favorable in the sight of God. The king on his throne, the murderer in his death cell, the queen in her boudoir, the harlot in her den of assignation, the philosopher in the hall of science, the peasant following the plow — all are in sin; all look alike to Christ. In the same way, upon the same conditions, applying in the same manner, they must be born again or each and every one of them will be forever doomed.

There are no mental restrictions. One does not need an unusual education, extreme knowledge, extraordinary talent, exceptional ability to become a Christian. The Gospel is the plain Word of God for plain people. The child, the underprivileged person, the benighted heathen — all may understand, believe, receive, be saved.

Some years ago, in a revival meeting in Natchitoches, Louisiana, on a Friday night, thirty-five people responded to the Gospel invitation and took their seats at the front of the auditorium. Among them was the head of the mathematics department of the Louisiana State Normal School, located in that city. In the same line was also a blacksmith by the name of Jess Brown. Night after night that blacksmith had raised his hand for prayer, but had refused every appeal to take his stand for Christ. That afternoon the pastor and I visited Brown in his "smithy." After some persuasion he declared that the thing that had kept him from a decision was his inability to read and write. He said he did not want to be embarrassed by being asked to fill out an application card. When the pastor promised to fill out the card for him he accepted Jesus and was received into church fellowship that night. These two men were poles apart, but Christ saved both of them.

There are no moral restrictions. The cry of God still is: *Though your sins be as scarlet, they shall be as white as snow; though they be red like crimson, they shall be as wool.* The blood of Jesus Christ, God's Son, still cleanses all sinners from all sin. Friends, you need not hesitate. No matter what your sin or sins may be, no matter how bleak or how black they may look to you, God is exceedingly, abundantly able to forgive above all that you ask or think. There is no stain so ingrained in your soul, there is no blemish so etched in your character, there is no habit so deeply driven into your conduct, but that Christ can save you from it, to the uttermost. The Devil has no hold upon you that the Son of God cannot break. Hell has no claim upon you that the blood of Christ cannot redeem. The law has no bill against you that the Redeemer has not fully satisfied.

There are no sex or age restrictions. Men, women, and children from the earliest days of accountability to the last hours of mortal existence, are all invited and welcomed by God. For nineteen hundred years men, women and children of every age, of every condition, of every clime, have found

a ready welcome in the open arms of the Son of God. Some
years ago on a Sunday night at the end of the closing service
of a revival, I was sitting in a great church. Exhausted,
dripping with perspiration, I watched the pastor baptize
the great number of candidates who had been saved and
added to the church during the campaign. In the course of
the baptismal service there stepped into the waters the
seventy-three-year-old manager of a large ice plant. Following him came the ten-year-old son of a deacon of that
church. Behind him came a Norwegian family, consisting
of a father, a mother, two sons and a daughter. The five
members of that family stood in the water while the pastor
baptized them, one after the other. Surely that scene was
ample proof of the universal offer of salvation insofar as
sex and age are concerned.

There is also in this text the universal condition of salvation. This too is simple, clear, definite, understandable. We
are not saved by our opinions, by our theories, by our
churches, by our ordinances, by our works, by our efforts.
We are saved by *Christ*. We must apply to Him for salvation. Our text states the universal condition of salvation in
these words: *whosoever shall call upon the name of the
Lord*. We are saved by calling upon the Name of the Lord.

What does that calling mean? What does it involve?
How must we call? The best illustrations of this calling
upon the Name of the Lord are, of course, found in Scripture. Understand the meaning in God's Word of that term
"call." We must rightly point out to you, then, the implications found in that condition.

There is first the call of repentant humility, the call of
sins grieved over and confessed, the call of transgressions
acknowledged and repented of. You no doubt recall the
story which Jesus tells in the eighteenth chapter of Luke,
beginning with the tenth verse: *Two men went up into the*

temple to pray; the one a Pharisee, and the other a publican. The Pharisee stood and prayed thus with himself, God, I thank thee, that I am not as other men are, extortioners, unjust, adulterers, or even as this publican. I fast twice in the week, I give tithes of all that I possess. And the publican, standing afar off, would not lift up so much as his eyes unto heaven, but smote upon his breast, saying, God be merciful to me a sinner. I tell you, this man went down to his house justified rather than the other: for every one that exalteth himself shall be abased; and he that humbleth himself shall be exalted. The Pharisee proudly boasted of his virtues, of his goodness, of his morality. The publican, in confessing his transgressions, humbled himself before the Lord, acknowledging his faults, admitting his sins, anxiously confessing his guilt. Jesus said, "This humble, penitent, confessing publican went home justified, a saved man."

Friends, you will never find favor with Christ, never obtain salvation until you first recognize your own unrighteousness and humbly admit it to God. There must be therefore the first call of repentance.

In the second place there is the call of faith for aid. Turn to the story of blind Bartimaeus, as recorded in the tenth chapter of Mark, beginning with the forty-sixth verse: *And they came to Jericho: and as he went out of Jericho with his disciples and a great number of people, blind Bartimaeus, the son of Timaeus, sat by the highway side begging. And when he heard that it was Jesus of Nazareth, he began to cry out, and say, Jesus, thou son of David, have mercy on me. And many charged him, that he should hold his peace: but he cried the more a great deal, Thou son of David, have mercy on me. And Jesus stood still, and commanded him to be called. And they call the blind man, saying unto him, Be of good comfort, rise; he calleth thee. And he, casting away his garment, rose, and came to Jesus. And Jesus answered and said unto him, What wilt thou that I should do unto thee? The blind man said unto him, Lord, that I might receive my sight. And Jesus said unto him, Go thy way; thy faith hath made thee whole. And immediately he received his sight, and followed Jesus in the way.* Bartimaeus was helpless in his blindness. He had almost, if not altogether, given up hope. From the remarks of passers-by he had heard of the mighty works of Jesus. When Christ came along and Bartimaeus knew who He was, there was no stopping him. When Christ passed by, Bartimaeus pressed on towards the only One who could give him relief. The passers-by strove to drive him back, but he continued to push forward. It perhaps took some time for Jesus to hear his cry, but Bartimaeus kept on calling. Why do you think Jesus asked him the question *What wilt thou that I should do unto thee?* Jesus knew that he was blind. Jesus knew that he wanted his sight restored. I believe this event shows us that the cry of faith is essential to salvation. Jesus paused, hesitated, waited. The minute Bartimaeus cried out in faith, *Lord, that I might receive my sight,* Jesus healed him with the words *Go thy way; thy faith hath made thee whole.*

There is last of all the call of grateful confession. Again and again it is referred to in Scripture. Stand with me on Calvary on the awful day of the Crucifixion. Hear once more the words recorded in Luke 23:39-43: *And one of the malefactors which were hanged railed on him, saying, If thou be Christ, save thyself and us. But the other answering rebuked him, saying, Dost not thou fear God, seeing thou art in the same condemnation? And we indeed justly; for we receive the due reward of our deeds: but this man hath done nothing amiss. And he said unto Jesus, Lord, remember me when thou comest into thy kingdom. And Jesus said unto him, Verily I say unto thee, To day shalt thou be with me in paradise.* I believe that the cry of the thief, *Lord, remember me when thou comest into thy kingdom,* was a confession of faith in the Lord Christ which insured salvation for that malefactor. Paul was on the road to Damascus, breathing out threatenings and slaughter. Christ met him, struck him to the ground and spoke to him: *Saul, Saul, why persecutest thou me?* I believe that when Paul asked, *Who art thou, Lord?* and upon hearing the answer of Jesus cried out, *Lord, what wilt thou have me do?* he was a saved man and became a child of God. Jesus said, *Whosoever therefore shall confess me before men, him will I confess also before my Father which is in heaven.* In our text we find this declaration of Paul's (Romans 10:9): *That if thou shalt confess with thy mouth the Lord Jesus, and shalt believe in thine heart that God hath raised him from the dead, thou shalt be saved.* The cry of confession is an absolute essential. If you believe Jesus is the Son of God, if you believe He died for your sins, if you love Him, if you trust Him, come today, take your stand for Him, confess Him before men. That is the least you can do after all He has done for you.

These three elements — repentance, faith, confession — must be present in our calling upon the Name of the Lord, ere we can be sure of the work of God unto salvation in our souls. Surely you can see the importance of each of the three elements. Surely they cannot constitute a barrier which causes you to hesitate about coming to Christ today. God cannot make this truth easier, simpler, more definite. Human language is incapable of expressing the truths of God in a clearer fashion. Call upon the Name of the Lord, in this very hour, and the power of God will do the rest.

The third thought in this text is the universal promise of salvation, contained in the words *shalt be saved.* This promise is rocklike in its positiveness. You need not dig around it or into it.

That promise is guaranteed by the absolute Word of God. In Numbers 23:19 we read: *God is not a man, that he should lie; neither the son of man, that he should repent: hath he said, and shall he not do it? or hath he spoken, and shall he not make it good?* God has never broken any promise He has made. He will not break this promise to you. You may depend upon it. You may step out upon it. You may build your life upon that rock. The eternal salvation of your soul, if you comply with God's condition, is guaranteed.

This promise is also supported by the finished work of Christ. The book of Hebrews states this definitely (Hebrews 9:12; 14): *Neither by the blood of goats and calves, but by his own blood he entered in once into the holy place, having obtained eternal redemption for us. For if the blood of bulls and of goats, and the ashes of an heifer sprinkling the unclean, sanctifieth to the purifying of the flesh: how much more shall the blood of Christ, who through the eternal Spirit offered himself without spot to God, purge your conscience from dead works to serve the living God?* When Jesus threw back His head against the Cross, looked up into the face of God, bowed His head and cried, *It is finished,* He had paid completely the due bill held against us by the law, by Satan, by sin. God would have to undo the work of Christ, the shame and agony of Calvary, would have to refill the veins of Jesus with the blood He shed that day before He could ignore anyone who called upon Him in the Name of the Crucified. Every drop of that precious ochre is an amen to the contention of Paul that *whosoever shall call upon the name of the Lord shall be saved.*

The testimony of the centuries, of the nineteen hundred years that have passed since the beginning of the proclamation of grace, is our sure foundation, is our solid hope, our certain faith in this promise. For nineteen hundred marvelous years uncounted multitudes of precious souls of every kind, of every condition, of every description, have been constrained to call upon the Name of the Lord. Not one of them has been lost. God has kept faith with every one of them. Their sins have been forgiven; their iniquities have been blotted out; their transgressions are remembered against them no more. Their souls have been regenerated, their affections renewed. They have joined the saintly band in ascribing glory and honor and praise to the Lamb of God which taketh away the sin of the world.

That is your hope, sinner. That is the way out of your sins. That is the path of the Cross that leads home to God and to heaven. Will you take it today? Will you call upon the Name of the Lord? Will you take your stand in the shadow of the bloodstained Cross? Will you look up into the face of God through the blood of His Son? Will you penitently in faith, boldly confess Him, your Saviour and Lord, crying, "For Jesus' sake, have mercy on me, a sinner"? God will reach down from heaven. He will apply the blood of His Son to your soul. He will take you out of the horrible pit, lift you out of the miry clay, put your feet on the Rock of Ages, put the song of Moses and of the Lamb upon your lips, start you on your way rejoicing, keep you, and finally receive you to Himself in glory where you shall sing His praises forevermore.

> Turn thee, O lost one, careworn and weary;
> Lo, the Good Shepherd is pleading today,
> Seeking to save thee, waiting to cleanse thee;
> Haste to receive Him; no longer delay.
>
> List to the message; think of His mercy!
> Sinless, yet bearing thy sins on the tree;
> Perfect remission, life everlasting,
> Through His atonement He offers to thee.
>
> Come in the old way, come in the true way;
> Enter through Jesus, for He is the Door;
> He is the Shepherd, tenderly calling;
> Come in thy weakness and wander no more.